Stephen's
MOON

For Stephen—you are safe in my heart and

my heart will go on.

For Stephanie and Ron—my lighthouse,

my strength, in the darkest days.

Stephen's MOON

Marcia H. Carter

Published by:
Black Sands Enterprises
Canton, Georgia
(770) 281-3101
http://www.blacksands.com

Cover and Interior Design:
Desktop Miracles, Inc.
Stowe, Vermont

Library of Congress Cataloging-in-Publication Data
Carter, Marcia H.
    Stephen's moon : a mother's journey through grief /
Marcia H. Carter.
    p. cm.
    ISBN 0-9671781-4-2
                              99-090631
                                 CIP

Table Of Contents

Acknowledgements

*S*pecial thanks to:

Charlie Walton and his book *When There Are No Words*, the book that saved me from myself.

Also to my grief counselor, Doug Lawson, who helped me through the tunnel.

Robert Wilson, my editor and my very dear friend.

Robert Pope, the cover artist.

And last, but not least, Kristin Swan—I can never thank you enough for what you did and continue to do.

CHAPTER ONE

The News

I always thought if something happened to one of my children, I would somehow know. I would feel it inside. If I were asleep, I would jolt awake with a horrible, heavy hearted, knowing feeling. I would pace the floor until the call came, confirming my fear. It would only be a matter of how it happened and then, the fear confirmed, I would fall onto the floor, screaming until everything went black and I died myself or the world ended.

But it didn't work that way. I slept. I slept all night, even though a horrible accident had happened at three A.M. I didn't find out about the accident until after ten o'clock the next morning. And when I did find out, I didn't die. The world didn't end. The sun just kept on unmercifully rising day after day.

I had remarried after being divorced for ten years and the address Stephen and I had shared had changed, but his driver's license hadn't been updated. I suppose the police went to an empty apartment to notify us of the horrible accident.

Stephen had a list of phone numbers in his wallet, numbers only, names weren't present. Since he knew to whom the numbers belonged, he apparently didn't feel that it was important to write the names. He was eighteen. Go figure.

I had told him to always have the home phone and my pager number with him. He said of course he did. And he did—toward the bottom of the list. Behind the girlfriend and the guys and the girls who were just friends. The police apparently grew tired of talking to kids in the middle of the night and quit long before they got to my pager number or the home phone.

The kids that the policemen called asking for next of kin were freaking out and calling the house at a frantic rate—but they were calling downstairs, to Stephen's private line—a phone we couldn't even hear ringing upstairs.

The call we received at ten the next morning was from the co-ordinator of the foreign exchange student board. Stephen had met a wonderful girl, Isabelle, who was an exchange student from Paris. Isabelle had stayed with this co-ordinator before being placed with a host *family*, which is why Stephen had the co-ordinator's number near the top of his list. Isabelle's host *family's* number was also near the top of the list, but they couldn't be reached that Sunday morning.

Everyone seemed to give up except this lady that I had never met. She didn't quit until she had Isabelle on the other end of the line. Isabelle gave her the upstairs phone number and the phone call was made, telling us that the police were looking for next of kin for Stephen Beam.

Ron, the wonderful man I had just married, took the phone call. The color drained from his face in front of my eyes. I asked what was wrong and he didn't answer. He took off downstairs to his office, next to Stephen's bedroom. I followed. He was dialing from the office phone. Urgent business on a Sunday morning? No. Business could never have put a look like that on his face. Not even if he had just lost his entire business.

With a pleading look on his face, he pushed the door shut behind him and began to talk quietly. I saw the message light blinking frantically on Stephen's extension at the computer just outside his bedroom and I walked to it. I flipped through caller ID and saw many familiar names, having called at very early hours. I couldn't get the messages, as Stephen had his own password.

"What is going on?" I demanded hysterically, walking back toward Ron's office.

He laid his head against the now partially opened door of his office, his green eyes full of tears. "Isabelle's co-ordinator says the police called her before daylight looking for next of kin for Stephen," he said in a voice that choked on the words. "I called the police and they say they don't have anything. I'm trying to find out what's going on."

"Find out now!" I heard myself scream, but he was already dialing again.

I was shaking. It was April 13th and very warm in the house, but I was cold. Horribly cold. Stephen was supposed to be spending the night with a friend. I walked back to his caller ID unit to confirm that the friend's name was among those having called before daylight. I shuddered as the number appeared. This wasn't a good sign. If Stephen would have called from the friend's house, he would have called on the upstairs line. I walked back to Ron's office and looked at him helplessly.

"I've left our number with the police and asked them to please look into it," Ron said in answer to my look as he frantically dialed yet another number.

It had to be a cruel hoax if the police didn't have anything, didn't it? Please let it be a cruel hoax.

I dialed the friend's number from Stephen's phone and didn't get an answer. I called my twenty five year old daughter, Stephanie, and begged her to tell me she had heard from Stephen. She hadn't seen him since ten thirty the night before.

The phone in Ron's office, idle for a second, rang. Ron grabbed it and took off upstairs, not seeming to believe what he was hearing. I followed. He went out onto the deck and closed the sliding glass door behind him. At this point, I knew I didn't want to know what they were saying, so I stayed in the kitchen.

The phone call was from the morgue. Stephen's body was there, an autopsy just completed. As the medical examiner gave a stammering Ron the exact cause of death, she realized that we hadn't even been notified of the accident. She apologized profusely, saying she had called the police station and asked for our number and it was given to her. Call me stupid, but this could not be standard procedure.

Maybe there is no ideal way to find out, but this was seriously lacking something. When Ron called the police station back, asking why no one knew what was going on, the policeman said there had been a shift change since the accident. Well, leave a sticky note.

Under the circumstances, I feel that every number on the list Stephen had should have been called until I was found. Ron has his own business at home, but also is a policeman second shift and if a child were to die on his shift, I know without him telling me, he wouldn't come home until he had up close and personally told those parents. I would expect no less of him.

Stephen had died at three A.M. in a single car accident. He couldn't sleep at his friend's house. Sleeping away from home had never been easy for him. When he was a child, I missed many episodes of *Dallas* because the phone call to pick him up usually came about that time on Friday night. I didn't mind. But now he could drive and he had left on his own.

He lost control of his little truck in a very bad curve, hitting a tree. The first witness on the scene was on foot, asking someone in a car to call 911. The wheels of the truck were still spinning as the people in the car called for help, then ran to the truck. The pedestrian disappeared. I will always feel that Stephen swerved to miss this pedestrian and lost control of his truck. Of course, I will never know.

Stephen had his seat belt on, the truck caved in on him. The steering wheel hit him just above the heart, severing his pulmonary artery and almost severing the aorta. He had died in less than a minute. An autopsy had been performed because Georgia law requires an autopsy on anyone under twenty one who dies suddenly.

When I went to bed on Saturday night, I had a healthy, beautiful eighteen year old son, whose most used line was, "Aw, Mama, you worry too much." When I awoke, that beautiful little boy was gone from me, his body battered by windshields, steering wheels and an autopsy.

It wasn't just the undecided, slightly reckless teen-ager I had to begin to try to give up. It was the infant who had lived in the world of Winnie the Pooh, who lay in my arms, taking his bottle, and when he saw me smiling at him, stopped taking the bottle and smiled back at me, the milk running out the corners of his mouth. It was the little boy who brought me flowers with a wonderful smile on his face when he was four, the arm with the flowers outstretched toward me, a cat named Charlie Bobby Sox tucked under his other arm.

It was the little league football player, smiling at me from under his helmet and giving me thumbs up, the twelve year old who cracked me up trying to bodysurf in Hawaii, the thirteen year old who had toured Europe with me, playing in the snow in the Alps. And yes, the eighteen year old, who outweighed me and towered over me, who had hugged me and comforted me just one short month earlier when he had served as pallbearer at my Dad's funeral.

I lost the baby, the little boy and the almost man—in one swift and fatal blow. I walked numbly back downstairs. I stood against the washing machine, trying to figure out how life could go on. I didn't want to call anybody because repeating it would make it more real. I sunk to the floor, the washing machine grazing my spine painfully as I went into a sitting position. I saw a pair of his dirty blue jeans in the laundry basket beside me. I embraced my knees, laid my head down, and rocked myself. "My baby," I sobbed. "My baby."

I seemed to rise from my broken body, much as Stephen must have risen from his broken body on his way to Heaven. I called my daughter because I knew I had to. Her husband answered and I heard him say over and over, "Oh, no. Oh, no, man." He was like a brother to Stephen.

Stephanie's voice was one of devastation, then, just as I did, she rose from her wrecked body and took it upon herself to drive to her dad's house in North Georgia to deliver the news.

Our TV had been playing before that horrible phone call came through, but no one was watching it. On my slow and painful ascent upstairs, I heard a news brief speaking of a horrible accident. When I reached the top of the stairs, I saw Stephen's little truck plastered on the TV screen, slices through the roof support posts of the cab a tell tale sign of the way his body had been retrieved. The name was being withheld pending notification of next of kin, the voice said, but I knew the other phone calls had to be made before all the other people who loved him saw the truck on TV. The news brief had been running every hour, if anyone would have been paying attention to the TV, we would have found out in yet another horrible way.

I called a friend. She was at church and her recorder picked up. I repeated the news to see how it sounded. It sounded horrible. I called my sister. She started crying and I stood like a zombie. I envied her having the ability to feel. I thought for a moment of my poor wrecked body down by the washing machine. But there was no time to think about that now. There were things I had to do.

Ron and my sister made the other phone calls and people started to come to the house. Some were surprised to see me cleaning a mirror or wiping off a counter. They would tell me to sit down. They didn't know that wiping the counter or cleaning the mirror gave me something to do with my life for the next five minutes and I couldn't think any further ahead than that.

Ron called the same funeral home that had handled my dad's funeral and arrangements were made for them to pick up Stephen's body at the morgue. We were to meet with them at four to make the arrangements for Stephen. All I could think about was my little boy's body in a cold morgue. "I want to go there. I need to be with him."

"No, you don't," people would say kindly. "He's in Heaven. That's just his body. You don't need to go there. You don't need to see him that way."

This wasn't happening.

I asked Ron to go by the tree Stephen had hit on the way to the funeral home. I had to make myself believe, so I stared at the scene. Stephen had hit the tree with the left front corner of the truck, the driver's side, the steering column becoming a battering ram to his heart. The left tire, wheel and all, was still lying against the tree. Why it hadn't been taken with the truck, I didn't know. The front grill was there, as well, and the inside console that had obviously been removed when the top was lifted off the truck. A yellow piece of plastic with some blood on it that his body had been placed on had also been discarded carelessly on the spot.

Cassette tapes were scattered, the brown tape spilling out of some of them. The strewn tape reminded me of when Stephen was a toddler and had gotten his hands on Stephanie's Madonna tapes, destroying them. I picked a tape up numbly. Confederate Railroad. *Jesus and Mama. Jesus and Mama always loved me*, the words came into my head. Guns N' Roses lay beside it. Metallica lay a step or two away.

A cracked plastic cassette case with names of songs recorded from Isabelle's CDs lay a little further down. The song titles were written in French in beautiful female penmanship. I picked up another tape with an assortment of songs that had been recorded from the radio. I had recorded them. Sam Cooke, Three Dog Night, Sammy Johns' *Chevy Van*, *Snoopy's Christmas* by the Royal Guardsman. Stephen had always laughed at Snoopy's Christmas battle with the Red Baron. All were songs that had been introduced to him by me. I remembered the fun we had had.

Fighting tears, I clutched the tapes in my hand and looked at the tree. A small pine tree. It didn't look big enough to do the damage that had been done. The bark was gone in the spot where the truck had hit and the tree was leaning. Beyond the tree, in the woods, lay his blue and white basketball. University of Kentucky. He had won it at Six Flags shooting baskets. He won one almost every time he played. The basketball had been catapulted from the back of the truck. I walked to it and picked it up, and clutching it close to me, along with the tapes, told my husband I was ready to go.

At the funeral home, I was told his body wouldn't be ready for viewing until the next morning. I remembered all the people who had assured me I didn't want to see him before the undertakers had their time with him. How bad was he? We made the funeral arrangements and went home and I went to my body beside the washer and cried.

CHAPTER TWO

Maybe When You're Eighteen

had been divorced since Stephen was eight years old. Stephanie was fourteen at the time of the divorce and very active with friends of her own, so Stephen and I were at home alone often. I remember one particular night, Stephen had fallen asleep on the sofa and I was watching a scary movie. As the suspense built, I slid back against the sofa and pulled Stephen's arm over my shoulder. I suppose it was a cowardly act, but deep down, I knew that I counted on his presence as much as he counted on mine.

He had asked me when he was fourteen if I was ever going to marry again. Stephanie had married and had just become the mother of twins when Stephen had asked the question.

"Maybe when you're eighteen," I answered. No one could hurt him if he was eighteen. No one could be a wicked stepfather. He would be too old.

"But, Mama," he said, "that's not fair to you."

The truth of the matter was I couldn't imagine a man treating me well, much less my children. I was happy and safe depending only on myself. I knew I would never let him down.

But I *had* let him down. I had let him lose his life. I sunk deeper into my crumpled body and cried more. I was riding around in a car with an airbag, his truck didn't have one. The phone rang and I spilled my thoughts to my friend on the other end.

"Please don't do this to yourself," she begged. She had lost her brother in an identical wreck in 1983 and was no stranger to the guilt. "My car doesn't have air bags, Marcia. I bought it five years ago, I like it, so I haven't traded. Please don't do this to yourself. The way he hit the tree," she cringed, "I don't think it would have mattered whether he had an airbag or not. And God doesn't make mistakes. If it wasn't his time to go, he wouldn't have gone."

This friend was the one I had called when I got the news of Stephen's death, the one who was at church. Maybe I had been reaching out to her from the very beginning to help me. I knew she had suffered loss.

She had come straight to my house when she received the horrible message and had tried from the moment she walked through the door to give me a lifeline. She was still trying as we talked now. She shared learned wisdoms with me. People say that nothing helps at a time like this, that there is nothing anyone can say to ease the pain, but that isn't true. Each caring word spoken, each little hint on how to survive is a lifeline thrown to you.

Of course, I wasn't able to grasp the lifeline yet, I was still in raging waters. But the lifeline was there, all the same. When we hung up, I forced my broken body to the next room and pulled out all my pictures of Stephen. I smiled at the one of him posing like a rock star in front of the Eiffel Tower. I looked at every picture of him from the time he was born as I sat with my broken body.

Ron came down and looked at some of the pictures with me and I knew he feared for my sanity, but he respected my wish to be alone, so I could stay with my broken body for the night.

"I put the gun in his hand," he said before going upstairs. "I bought him that truck."

"No. You loved him and you were good to him. You bought him the truck because he needed it." I thought *his* guilt was preposterous, but I didn't think mine was.

I stared at the tapes that had been retrieved from the crash site. Stephen's versatility in music had always amazed me. He loved it all. Country to hard rock and everything in between. "What would the world be like without music?" I heard him ask and I thanked God I could still hear his voice in my head.

I turned the Metallica tape in my hand and I remembered his words about Isabelle. "She's so cute," he had said in a voice that sounded like he was cooing over a baby. "She's from Paris and Mama—do you know how she says Metallica?"

"How?" I had asked, trying not to laugh.

"She says Me-tal-e-ca."

"Really?" I asked, amused that he was making a complete idiot of himself over a girl. He had always played it so cool, I had never imagined this.

I laid the tape down and looked at the Confederate Railroad tape.

"Look at that bus. It's Confederate Railroad's bus!" I heard him say.

"Who?" I had asked.

He had told me who they were and had played their songs for me. For the past four years, each and every time he got into any kind of trouble with me, he would turn his head sideways and sing the one line—*Jesus and Mama always loved me* and he would find himself immediately cleared. Even when he brought a black lab puppy home to our very small apartment.

Guns N' Roses. Axl Rose. Stephanie and Stephen loved Guns N' Roses. I had heard them since 1988. But I had never really listened until the early nineties. Stephen always respected my music and I tried to show the same respect.

"Listen to this song," I heard him say.

The song was *Sweet Child 'O Mine* and Axl was doing his thing, his famous whine. *Sweet child 'o mine-ine-ine-ine-ine.*

"It's distinctive," I said. It was as close to a compliment as I could think of at the moment. I hoped it would suffice.

I walked the few steps to Stephen's tape player and put the tape in. I found that Axl's trademark *I-I-I-I-* whine that I had come to appreciate had become a painful wail, an unfathomable cry of pain. Axl seemed to be suffering right along with me. I loved Axl even more for it. I let the pain engulf my broken body, it echoed to the depths of my soul.

"*Where do we go/Where do we go?*" the song asked.

"Oh, dear God where do *I* go from here? Where do I go without Stephen?" I asked, sinking to the floor in another outburst of tears. I still needed him, I still depended on him as much as he did me and I always would have.

I remembered Stephen in November of 1992, fourteen years old, running out onto the patio with an empty two liter Coke bottle and holding it out into the rain. The bottle half filled, he brought it back inside. "November rain," he smiled, placing the bottle in his room.

"What?" I had asked, a little puzzled.

"Listen to this song," he said in explanation. "It's tragic, but it's so pretty."

Nothing lasts forever, not even cold November rain, I heard the lyrics in my head.

November Rain would be played at his funeral, I decided at that moment, pulling myself back together. There would be a lot of conflict with this, I knew. Southern Baptist preachers and rock and roll didn't mix, but this was no time to worry about the preachers.

I remembered as a child listening to *Up, Up, and Away* by the Fifth Dimension in my room at home. It was a brand new song and I loved it. My mother was in the living room, dusting, when she happened to look out the window and see the pastor of our church turning in. She was—horror of horror—wearing shorts. She went running through the house, telling me to turn the music off and to go let the preacher in while she changed clothes.

I never understood this. Our house had no air conditioning, it was hot. I saw nothing wrong with her wearing shorts. It was *our* house. I also didn't think it was any of the preacher's business if I played my radio in my room. And for the record, I felt that it was rude to drop in without a phone call.

Of course, I was twelve years old and my opinion didn't carry a lot of weight, so I didn't open my mouth. I turned the radio off, opened the door for him, my mother changed clothes and we offered him some tea.

This was not an isolated event. It happened many times. I'm sure the man experienced some close encounters with rock `n roll in my front yard. As I said, there was no air conditioning and my windows were always up.

One time, my mother was in the yard in her shorts working on her flowers when he turned in and she didn't have time to change clothes. He preached about women wearing shorts and causing men to lust the following Sunday morning.

I changed churches when I was old enough, but didn't come out a lot better. I still heard the sermons on music and Hell and how women led men to lust by wearing shorts. I truly in my heart did not feel that God disapproved of my music or cared if I wore shorts, so I had a hard time with these sermons. Who were the preachers to be above God?

Twenty four years after the summer I refer to, this same preacher was out visiting. He knocked on my door and introduced himself. I smiled at his devotion, even though we didn't see eye to eye. I told him who I was and he asked about my parents.

Stephen was fourteen and in his room playing Guns N' Roses. I didn't ask him to turn it off, it was our house. Out of curiosity, Stephen did turn the music off and came out to see who was in our living room. I introduced him to the preacher.

Stephen had always been confused with religion, telling me that he couldn't get into it like I did. I had at this point in time, found a bigger, more liberal Baptist church, and was very happy, but Stephen still had a hard time with it.

I always told him he was lucky to have such a liberal church available and shared with him the horror stories of my youth. He simply said he couldn't have put up with what I did and asked me if I had ever considered the possibility that the preacher had been trying to catch my mother in her shorts for his own entertainment.

I had laughed at his honesty and considered the possibility. He laughed now, amused that he had met the man who had tried to catch his grandmother in her shorts.

The preacher, with concern in his very soul for Stephen, came back to our house the next week. I was at work, Stephen was at home alone. This very man, this preacher, the hater of shorts and music was the one to get through to Stephen and I will never understand it, but I will always love him for it.

17

Stephen called me and told me about the visit. I was apprehensive, but Stephen said he understood more now and he had accepted Jesus. I was sure the preacher had threatened him with the fires of Hell and had scared salvation into him, but Stephen said no, they had just talked. The Lord truly does work in mysterious ways.

So, under the circumstances, this preacher had been called on immediately to officiate Stephen's funeral—it seemed very fitting. After all, he was the one who had the burden for my son's soul and had done the follow up visit. But—I was going to play Guns N' Roses? I checked my guts and found that I had enough.

This was the last thing I could do for my son, my son who was very up front and never hypocritical. He loved Guns N' Roses and he loved God. It's not an impossibility. I know that the lifestyle of Guns N' Roses is not a good example to kids, but neither were the deacons who drank themselves into a stupor when they went deer hunting and fell out of tree stands when I was a kid. As soon as they could walk again, they would get in the pulpit and condemn drinking and rock and roll. Things leak, guys. We're not impressed.

The members of Guns N' Roses don't pretend to be saints, that's for sure. It doesn't make what they do right, I'm not saying that, but hypocrisy chokes me. And I wouldn't be a hypocrite and not stand up for what my son would have wanted. The lyrics to *November Rain* are truly beautiful and they would be played.

I knew I had to leave my broken body and go upstairs and try to sleep for a couple of hours, but I didn't want to.

18

My son's body was cold and alone in a room at the funeral home. I flinched and looked at one more picture. Stephen was eight or nine in the picture and a memory sprang to my mind. "Can you see the moon?" he had asked as we drove home from my parents' house one night.

"Yes," I had answered, taking my eyes away from the road and looking into the sky.

The sky was a beautiful dark blue and perfectly clear, not a cloud in sight. A few scattered stars dotted the heavens, but none around the moon. It hung boldly alone in the sky, almost full, not quite, and it stood out like silver against the dark blue sky, so clearly that the craters on it seemed to be raised.

"It looks like a quarter falling from God's pocket," Stephen said and I thought it was the most profound thing I had ever heard.

I had gasped at the accurate description and was sure that he would be a famous writer or something someday. I kissed the picture that evoked the memory. "Stephen's moon," I said, still looking at the little boy in the picture as I rose once again from my broken body. That moon, the almost full moon on a clear night, would always be Stephen's moon to me.

I went to bed and slept fitfully for a little while. I was afraid of waking up and having the relieved feeling that I had *dreamed* he was dead. Realizing that it wasn't a dream would be too cruel, like reliving the news.

But, I found that even in my dreams, I knew he was dead. I dreamed someone was trying to take my pictures of him and it was a nightmare. Then I dreamed the pictures were out in the rain and I was trying to collect them before they were ruined, but there was a fence with no gate and I couldn't get to them. I managed to climb over the fence, but it was dark and I screamed for someone to turn on a light, but no one would. I groped for the pictures in the dark, grabbing what I could, then awoke in a sweat.

The phone rang a couple of hours later and the funeral director asked for more time. He said they had worked late into the night, but he still needed more time. Everything in my body cringing, I told him he could have all the time he needed.

He also verified the spelling of the family members' names for the article in the paper.

CHAPTER THREE

He Is Survived By

More than once I had wondered why the obituaries read this way. It sounded as if there had been a boating accident and some of the people on board had made it and others drowned.

Today I understood quite well why the obituary read the way it did. It was a matter of survival, not from going under water literally, but figuratively keeping your head above water after having your heart ripped out by the loss of the one who didn't make it.

We walked into the room, the room where Stephen lay quietly in the coffin we had chosen the day before. We were instructed not to touch his forehead. Plastic was involved. I wanted to scream, but didn't.

Looking at him was the first step to closure, I was sure, but what a horrible, horrible thing it was. There was no mistake, they were right, this accident had really happened and Stephen had really died. He was lying in front of me in the suit we had bought him just a month earlier for Daddy's funeral. He had looked so good in it, clowning from behind his shades. Now he was so pale and so still. A near scream followed by sobs went up from his real father and tears fell silently from Stephanie.

"Where's his hair?" I asked stoically.

"It's tucked under him," the funeral director said kindly.

I remembered a few years ago when Stephen had let his hair grow long and I hadn't liked it. I had come to accept it very quickly because I realized how much it meant to him. Thank God I had respected him enough to let it be. What a petty, petty thing it would have been to alienate him from me over something like that. "I want his hair out on his shoulders," I said.

"OK," the funeral director nodded and he reached carefully behind the seemingly sleeping face and pulled the hair out from behind him and let it fall on his shoulders. I knew he was being careful because the back of Stephen's head had been involved in the autopsy.

"Where are his earrings?" I asked. I also hadn't been a fan of the earrings at first, but had grown to accept them, as well.

"He wasn't wearing any," the funeral director said. "I'll check with the medical examiner's office."

I saw Ron say something quietly to the funeral director and he nodded. I somehow knew, without hearing, that they were saying the earrings might have been knocked from his ears during the crash.

I flinched. The weeping continued from the others, but I didn't cry. I am a very private person and sharing my grief was something I couldn't do. This was too deep for tears and it was between Stephen and me. Only Stephen would know how badly I was hurting. No one else would have a clue. No one else could possibly know the significance the child had in my life. It was more than a mother son relationship. It was years and years of depending on each other with no father figure involved.

I felt both of us had been cheated. He hadn't had a carefree childhood and now, when things were really good for both of us, he was gone. I waited until everyone was out of the room and I could stand at the coffin alone.

He looked older than eighteen because his pimples were covered by makeup. His left eyebrow was fake, a lot of his forehead was fake. I touched his hands, his arms, his sweet little face, my heart aching that he was so cold and so hard. I looked at the left hand that I knew by heart. I rubbed the little scar that had been there since he was six or seven. I always thought he had burned it with a lighter, but he never admitted to it.

The scar brought to mind the days he questioned everything I told him he couldn't do. I told him that one day he would have a child called Stephen 'Bo Jackson' Beam and then when he was a father, he would understand why I wouldn't let him do certain things.

He approved of the name for his child and constantly asked me what else little Stephen Bo would do. When he starting going out with Isabelle, I had teased him, asking did this mean that his child's name would be Stefan Beau

23

Jackson Beam. He laughed heartily because we hadn't talked about little Stephen Bo in years.

It didn't hit me full force until three hours later, as Isabelle stood beside the coffin, crying, that there would never be a little Stephen Bo or Stefan Beau. I went to the bathroom and cried in a stall.

My way of grieving may sound strange, but it's the way I am. If I burst into tears in a crowded room and people rush to comfort me, I smother. I don't want it. I'll stop crying just to get them to leave me alone and the pain stays inside. One to one with my husband or my daughter is quite different. But sometimes, I didn't even want that. It was truly a grief too deep for words, too deep to share. Absolutely no one except Stephen could know the extent of my pain. Many people find comfort in being hugged and helped, which is perfectly OK. People grieve differently and they must be allowed to grieve in their own way. Mine was between Stephen and me.

I began to wonder if the medical examiner was right. Did Stephen die as fast as they said? Or did he hurt? The damage to his face was obvious and the internal injuries were even worse. Was there blood all over his truck from the wounds? Head wounds bled so much, even little ones.

I sat down in a corner of the room to try and breathe. Did the people on the scene think no one cared about him because my number wasn't readily available? The thought killed me inside. Did Stephen have time to think, to know that he was dying?

I knew that wherever he was right now, he missed me. He was feeling the pain of separation just as I was. And he knew no one could understand the depth of what he was feeling except me. My mother disagreed with me. She said that in Heaven there was only happiness and that he didn't miss me. But I knew that he did. It wasn't a conceited thought, I just knew.

I thought again of his struggle with religion, his doubts. What if he wasn't in Heaven after all? When I was his age, I was sure if I died I would go to Hell. I wished for a purgatory so badly, I wanted to become Catholic. I needed some gray area, some in-between spot to adjust from this life to the next.

I saw a girl with blonde hair walk down the hallway, holding an ivory rose. I wondered who she was. She seemed older than most of Stephen's friends, closer to Stephanie's age. And she looked extremely nervous. She went into the bathroom, then came out and entered the room. "Are his parents here?" she asked in a voice that was very near shaking.

I stood. "I'm his mother."

"You're the one," she muttered as if to herself and tears came to her eyes. "You're the one."

She seemed to be choking on tears and I tried to assure her without words that whatever she needed to say she could.

"You'll think I'm crazy," she said.

"No, I won't."

Her name was Kristin, she and her fiancée were the passengers in the car that had come upon the accident, the one the pedestrian had asked to call for help. The wheels of the truck still spinning, the headlights shining into the woods, the call was placed and she took off down the small hill toward the truck and jumped into the back. The windows were shattered and she reached in and put her arms around my son.

"I knew the minute I touched him that he was a loved little boy. I knew someone somewhere was going to be devastated," she choked. "I knew that just by touching him."

With those words she dispelled my fear that the people on the scene thought no one cared about him because my number wasn't readily available.

She said that another man stopped and tried to do CPR, but to no avail. She kept saying in an emotional voice that Stephen looked like a teenager who had been knocked out, they couldn't believe he was dead.

She believed only when she felt a divine presence very near her. A divine presence and a sense of peace like she had never in her life felt, an experience that changed her life forever. There was no longer any doubt in my mind that Stephen was in Heaven. Forget that fear.

At the same time she felt the angel, she also heard a voice in her head say, *Find her. Tell her that it wasn't a bloody scene, tell her I'm where I'm supposed to be.* Sweet little Stephen. So worried that he got a message to me even after he was gone.

"You're the one he was talking about. I knew it when I saw you. Please don't think I'm crazy," she said, wiping a tear.

I could hardly think she was crazy when she had just answered the exact questions that were driving me crazy. I hugged her. "Thank you. Thank you for being there."

"I hope you aren't angry that I touched him. One of my friends told me that you could sue me for that."

Angry? Sue her? Never in a million years. "I could never thank you enough for what you did and for what you have just told me." I would always love her for having her arms around him, for being with him when I couldn't be.

"After the paramedics and police got there, there was nothing to do but wait for the equipment," she flinched, looking apologetically at me, "to get there to get him out of the truck. I asked the police if I could go to my apartment and call every number on the list that they had taken from his wallet until I found you, but they wouldn't let me. I would have found you. I wouldn't have stopped until I found you. I knew how important it was, Stephen had made that clear, but the police didn't know how important it was."

Apparently they didn't. They hadn't done such a hot job. My number was on that sheet of paper. If they felt that it was too much trouble to call all the numbers, they should have let Kristin.

I introduced her to Stephanie and very touched, we walked to the coffin with Kristin and she placed the ivory rose next to Stephen.

"What happened to his head?" Kristin asked immediately, seeing the makeup and the fake eyebrow. I thought it a strange question coming from her, but came to understand rather quickly.

"I was told the windshield came in on him," I said.

She nodded, saying that the truck had caved in, that her arm was against the console as she held him, she couldn't even see the steering wheel, but that there was no cut, no blood. "I touched him all over his face trying to get him to wake up, I had no blood on my hands."

Her fiancée clarified that from his position beside the window of the truck, he could see the cut, a fleshy gaping cut with no blood. Could one really bleed to death internally that fast? The implication took my breath away, but also let me know that Stephen didn't suffer. The impact had to have knocked him out and he never regained consciousness. My poor baby.

Kristin left, saying she would be back later and I sat down, longing to be in my broken body at home by the washer. I was very thankful for Kristin's coming forward, so thankful for all she had told me, so thankful that Stephen hadn't suffered, so amazed that he had imprinted such a powerful message on her that she had sought me out, but so devastated at my loss.

CHAPTER FOUR

Flo, Bessie, Gertrude and Old Rufus

I remembered going to funerals as a child, horrified at the end of the ceremony when the coffin was opened and everyone walked around one last time. You knew that as it got closer and closer to the front row where the family sat, the cries would get worse. Then came the screaming, the fainting, the hanging onto the coffin, the coffin rocking. My eyes must have almost popped out of my head. Then everyone went home and talked about who took it hard and who didn't.

At the age of seven, I had been pretty upset to learn that old Gertie never really loved Rufus. I had been certain that she had. I had seen them together and they had really been having some good times. And the way they looked at each other was so nice.

I was sure fooled, I guess, because after old Rufus' funeral, the adults said that Gertie didn't *take on* enough. She just walked around zombie like the whole time, they said. At the funeral home, she greeted guests like she was the hostess, not a grieving widow. Another said she bet old Rufus had a lot of life insurance and Gertie was probably glad he was gone. My mouth fell open. Why, that devil Gertie!

"Bessie and Flo must have really loved him," I said to the adults. "Bessie screamed and tried to climb in the coffin with him and Flo passed out cold."

"They were putting on," I was told simply.

How in the world did these adults know all this? How could they tell who was *putting on* and who meant it and who grieved enough and who didn't? They sure were smart. I couldn't tell.

I dreaded the day when I would face this because I truly did love people and I was sure I would scream, cry, lie on the coffin and faint. After all, that was what you did when you loved someone, according to these adults.

As the longest day of my life unfolded, I remembered poor old Gertie. Maybe her poor broken body had been at home by her washing machine, too. I don't think she had a washing machine, though. So maybe it was by the fireplace or in Rufus' chair in the living room.

The guests poured in and I greeted them like a hostess, touched and truly thankful to them for sharing in my grief and my loss. I was the zombie at times, not remembering who I had spoken to about what. Poor, poor Gertie, I thought again.

Just as Gertie was doing all those years ago, I was dealing with this loss on a much more personal level than anyone in the building. I had to deal with it the best way I could. And my way was the right way for me.

CHAPTER FIVE

Everyone's a Genius or a Saint

The flowers began to pour in, filling the room Stephen was in and the adjoining empty room. Every single flower that came through the door was a symbol of someone's love for Stephen. I had never before had a clue just how much flowers meant at the time of a death.

Although donations are wonderful and help much needed organizations in the name of the deceased, I knew that I would never again make *just* the donation. I left the funeral home that night feeling that all the flowers around Stephen were like a blanket of love, that he wasn't really alone in that room.

I spent another sleepless night in my broken body by the washer and made a trip to the medical examiner's office the next morning to pick up personal effects that hadn't been released to the funeral director. We went from there to the wrecker service where the truck had been towed to look for the missing earrings.

"Wait here," Ron said, but of course, I didn't.

I faced the crumpled truck face to face. The steering wheel was jammed into the seat so hard, Ron had to pry it back with a two by four so Stephanie and I could look for the earrings. The steering wheel—the inanimate object that had killed my son. I hated the steering wheel. I felt extreme compassion for people who had lost loved ones to murder. It would be hard not to take matters into your own hands when a living, breathing person had taken the life of a loved one.

As I looked in the floor for the earrings, I saw Stephen's shoes. Bluish gray canvas Airwalks. I wondered if he had been thrown out of them or if the paramedics had pulled him out of them. One shoe was doubled over, crumpled in the metal that had caved in around the gas pedal and the brakes. I felt myself choking.

"There's one earring," I heard Ron say, still retracting the steering wheel. "It's in the seat."

Stephen's favorite earring. I took it in my hand. Stephanie insisted on freeing the shoe. Ron held the steering wheel while she struggled with all her might, finally releasing the shoe from the metal. She clutched both shoes in her arms, her body shaking, and we left. We drove back to the funeral home, and I gave the earring to the funeral director and watched him place it in Stephen's ear.

I looked at the little body that really wasn't so little anymore and pain flooded my soul again. I wondered again if his feet had been in the shoes or if he had been thrown from them. His right foot would have shattered if it had been in the shoe, I cringed. I realized that he was dead and maybe it sounded crazy to worry about whether his foot was broken or not, but I did. If the earrings had been knocked from his ears, he was more than likely knocked out of his shoes, I told myself.

I was touched on the back and turned to see an old friend. I smiled, grateful to see her. "Was he wearing his seat belt?" she asked. Thinking silently to myself that there were better things to say right now, I simply nodded. "Do you think if he'd had an air bag, he would have lived?" she asked next.

I couldn't even address that question. I'm not a violent person, but I wanted to sock her one right between the eyes. *I'm so sorry* would have been a much better thing to say. Why would anyone ask such a stupid thing at a time like this? Did she feel my guilt was not sufficient or was she just stupid?

I had been told that Stephen couldn't have survived either way. I didn't know, nobody knew. Some people had speculated that if he hadn't had his seatbelt on, perhaps he would have been thrown clear of the steering wheel. Others were of the opinion that if he hadn't had the seatbelt on, he would have been thrown through the windshield and, at best, would have been a vegetable.

Who really knows *what if? What ifs* accomplish nothing at this point in time. I chose to believe that God had called Stephen and that God didn't make mistakes. Death was irreversible and I had to learn to accept it. Feeling that God had taken him for a good reason was better than elaborating on airbags and seatbelts and what ifs.

The next stupid statement came from another friend who told me that God had taken my child because He knew I could handle it, that He would never take hers because He knew she couldn't handle it. I almost crumbled when she said that. Did she think she loved her child more than I had loved mine? Did *God* think she loved her child more than I did mine?

The simple truth of the matter, of course, is that this very same thing *could* happen to her and she *would* have to handle it the same way anyone does—one agonizing breath at a time. And maybe in a backward way, she had been trying to compliment my strength, not meaning it in a bad way, but I took it badly.

By the same token, maybe the friend who had asked all the questions about the seatbelt and the airbag was trying to find a *reason* why Stephen had died. People need reasons so they can feel in control and therefore prevent this kind of tragedy happening to them or their children. She has a son the same age as Stephen and maybe she was terrified by what had happened and thought if she dotted all her i's and crossed all her t's, this kind of thing could never happen to her son. She would make sure he had an airbag, she would drill into his head to wear his seatbelt. This, of course, doesn't guarantee anything, but it was probably the reasoning behind her questions.

But I wasn't in the mood to be generous and console her fears. I didn't want those questions asked of me. Tell someone else what you're thinking, not the one mourning her child.

The day was far from over. Yet another older, religious acquaintance of my parents told me God had taken Stephen because I had divorced my ex husband and God was punishing me, that God did not accept divorce. I could not find any excuse for his words, no matter how hard I tried. He said that adultery was the only reason God accepted divorce and my ex had only hit me, not committed adultery. *Only?* I was beginning to think I served a totally different God than the one they spoke of. The God I knew had never condoned the way I was treated in the marriage.

And then there was the criticism of the music. Some members of my ex husband's family who found out that I planned to play Guns N' Roses had to have their say. These, of course, are the same people who didn't have anything to say in my defense when my ex was leaving bruises on my face. They saw nothing wrong with that; however, they felt they must stand up for what was *right* as far as the music was concerned because they were such good Christians.

I received angry, holier than thou lectures and advice from them which was ignored. Other church members thought I had lost my mind as well, although they weren't as vocal about it. But this was no time to change clothes and turn the radio off 'cause the preacher had turned in— the music was gonna play this time, by God.

This was my son and it was the last thing I could do for him and it was appropriate and it would be done. I personally, would feel like a cold, uncaring person going into a funeral home where someone was grieving over a loved one and opening my mouth to criticize anything. Criticizing would be more unchristian than any music that could possibly be played.

People in mourning are not in a good mood anyway, so words should be kind. I know it's hard to know the right thing to say, maybe there is no right thing to say, but the few mentioned above are definitely bad material.

I went home to my broken body and sobbed profusely, these people went home and slept so they'd be alert and ready to criticize the next day at the funeral.

CHAPTER SIX

If They Knew
What We Know . . .

The next morning on the way to the funeral home, we were passed by a carload of teenagers, speeding. I shuddered. "If they knew what we know, they wouldn't be driving like that," I said.

They turned on their blinker and turned in at the funeral home. "Apparently, they do," Ron said as we turned in behind them and watched them get out of the car, some of them weeping.

Teenagers think they are invincible, it's a known fact. I know I did. I got behind the wheel at sixteen loaded with inexperience and immaturity, but thinking I knew it all. I made mistakes. I found out how easily a car slides in the rain. I found out that when it rains hard, leaves fall onto the road and your car tires are at a loss for traction when they hit the wet leaves. I found out that different cars handle differently. I found out I was taking a curve too fast when the tires squealed and I went onto the wrong side of the road. I was lucky. I didn't die learning these things.

My heart pounded each time and I said a hasty prayer of thanks that there had been no oncoming traffic or that I hadn't left the road and hit a tree or telephone pole *and* that my parents hadn't seen me do it. The next time, I knew from experience how to avoid the situation. I slowed down. Some teenagers aren't that lucky.

I had spent a year with a learner's license, I had taken driver's education, but let's face it, when you're finally in a car without your mom or dad or your instructor, it's a whole different ballgame and not always because you're rebellious or wild. In my case, my mom and dad made me drive so slowly in the learning phase, I never came close to sliding on rain slickened streets or leaves. Had we hit an oil slick the size of Georgia, I would have crept right on through it. Most people thought I was seventy years old, I drove so slowly.

In driver's education, the same applied. We sometimes reached the speed limit, but never accidentally found ourselves going five or ten miles over as one might do alone. You see, the teacher had a brake and a certain look he gave. And as for all the reading material, it teaches how driving should be done, but cannot teach experience or maturity.

Stephen had never been anxious to drive or to have a car of his own. He was a far cry from my daughter who had to have her license the day she turned sixteen. He got his license after his eighteenth birthday. He loved the little truck Ron bought him and he loved the freedom it gave him, but he was by no means a show off or a daredevil.

He was almost a timid driver, but nonetheless, he was an invincible teenager. Once his license was in his pocket, he didn't like the corrections that were still coming from me or anyone else who chose to ride with him. He would point out quickly that he had his license, he could drive.

This time, he had gone into a curve too fast. Inexperience, not recklessness. He was also accustomed to a camper being on his truck. It had been taken off so he could move a bedroom suite. It made the truck lighter and this may have played a part in his failure to regain control. As I said, there's so much that one has to *learn* about driving a car. More than books can teach.

Although there's so much a teenager in a car doesn't know it could fill a book, you could never convince the teenager of that. Maturity can't be taught, it has to be acquired. Dangerous road conditions can't be totally explained, they have to be experienced.

In all honesty, as adults, we sometimes feel pretty invincible, too. We don't think it can happen to us. It does happen to adults, but nowhere near as frequently as it happens to Stephen's age group. Car accidents are the number one killer of eighteen to twenty five-year olds. Our driving experience saves us sometimes, teenagers don't have that advantage. We were lucky enough to gain our experience without dying and we learned from it.

The first question presented to me once inside the funeral home was whether or not I was angry with my son for wrecking. I thought it a preposterous question. I wished some of these people with no sense would just stay home. I replied that of course, I wasn't angry. They didn't believe me, said I must be angry, it was dark, he was an inexperienced driver, he took the curve too fast. He had no recovery time when he lost control, whether he lost control because of the pedestrian or not.

I couldn't imagine being angry with him and I told the person as much. Stephen made a mistake. He went into the curve too fast, no argument. But if everyone who made a mistake or a miscalculation died because of it, there would be no one here to talk about it.

People were flowing through the front doors and the two rooms were becoming packed as the time for the funeral grew near. I looked into kind, sad faces. For every person who angered me, there were a hundred exact opposites who would do anything they could to help with no judgement and no criticism.

A friend from church walked toward me. "Any time of the day or night you need me, you call me," she said. I nodded gratefully. She had found out about the accident on Monday morning and she had come to the funeral home immediately, her hair pulled back, soaking wet because she hadn't taken the time to dry it.

She had hugged me that first day and said nothing. I remembered attending her son's funeral two short years before. Another automobile accident. Another young life. No words were needed between the two of us. She was well aware of the horrible journey I had just embarked on.

The others from church stood in a rigid line, their hearts broken. Most of them were from the singles department, where I had spent many years. We had prayed together before—for a single dad with a brain tumor, for sick children. I knew they prayed for me now.

The pianist left the room to go to the chapel and start the music, the pianist who had told me that she would play anything I wanted. We had decided to leave Guns N' Roses strictly to Axl and the CDs, but it meant a lot to me that she had offered.

The funeral director stood solemnly at the door and I looked around the room one last time. So many young people, so many relatives, so much grief. I saw my cousin, Debbie, in the adjoining room. She gave me a supportive smile. It seemed she had been here the entire time. I had never looked around without seeing her. Many times she had been sitting with my long time friend, Billie Jean, the two of them sharing their devastation and seeming to try blindly, desperately, to plot a strategy for my survival.

My cousin Billy, Debbie's younger brother, stood before me now, giving me a message from a pall bearer who was running late. Billy has the most beautiful eyes known to mankind and as I looked up into them, I had a vivid flashback of our childhood. I saw Debbie pretending to marry Elvis in our yard, my sister Wanda a part of the ceremony with Ricky Nelson beside her. And then, I would enter, marrying Richard Chamberlain, Billy laughing at our fantasies as he looked on with those same blue eyes.

These might have been memories one would have smiled about, but they sent a chill down my spine. We were together years before Stephen was born and here we all were, still together, pulling together, to lay Stephen to rest. This wasn't fair to Stephen. I knew it was a form of survivor's guilt, but I felt hysteria rising.

I knew the term *survivor's guilt* well. Stephen had lost a classmate in fourth grade. The child was murdered and Stephen had a hard time dealing with it. Each time Stephen and I would drive to a movie or Lake Lanier Islands or Six Flags, he would ask to go by his friend's grave on the way. As we would sit beside the grave, he would say, "It's not fair. Josh can't go to the lake or the movies or Six Flags."

Counselors told me it was called peer survivor's guilt. I had a feeling that *peer* survivor's guilt would be far surpassed by *parental* survivor's guilt. I knew that what I was feeling right now was only the tip of the iceberg and the hysteria rose closer to the surface. My uncle, Debbie and Billy's dad, his face strained and full of grief, swallowed hard as he looked over my head once more at Stephen's peaceful face and he put a comforting hand on my shoulder. He said nothing, but my hysteria went back to its place and I remembered that my broken body was at home by the washer.

His wife, my aunt, stood quietly beside him. I had never seen the fiery little lady so quiet in all my life. She looked as if the breath had been violently knocked from her body and she couldn't regain it. I knew her quietness would be a thing of the past if someone dared voice a word of disapproval of the music within her earshot. If need be, she would willingly do battle for what I wanted for my son.

The funeral was beautiful and the songs were beautiful. Not a one of my sixty and seventy year old aunts, to their credit, voiced a bad word about the music, although they are as Christian or more so than anyone in the building. Their standard funeral songs are *Amazing Grace* and *Just a Rose Will Do,* just the same as the people who had complained, but each and every one of them stood firmly behind me on the music.

Kids openly sobbed when the music began. It was so Stephen. The preacher of my youth tapped his foot and bore with us, although his blood pressure probably rose considerably. The other preacher in attendance asked that the music be stopped. The funeral director didn't oblige. Stephen's funeral won't go down as one of the top ten Baptist funerals of all time, but that wasn't my goal.

Two of my aunts loved Guns N' Roses and wanted to know where they could obtain a copy. I would have laughed under different circumstances. One aunt told me that she had never heard more appropriate music at a funeral. She was right.

The last words having been spoken, a long line of cars followed the shiny blue hearse to the outskirts of Kennesaw Mountain National Park to a cemetery called Cheatham Hill, where Stephen was placed in a mausoleum. One hundred and twenty three years earlier, a Civil War battle had raged on these slopes.

I remembered Stephen as a child playing around the cannons just down the street. He would pretend to fire the cannon, then take cover as the imaginary Yankees drew ever closer. This wasn't real, my mind told me suddenly. That little boy who played Civil War couldn't be gone.

I had things to do. I once again told myself that I couldn't worry about my broken body at home by the washer. Many people were coming to the house. There were things I had to do. The people came, the people left. Now what?

CHAPTER SEVEN

Healing the Broken Body Down by the Washer

I was in a sea of despair and I was struggling to keep my head above water. I couldn't swim and couldn't imagine ever learning how. I knew that people were throwing me a lifeline and that my only hope was to have a raft. One could never learn to swim in this kind of water.

Stephen's jeans and other clothes still lay in the basket by the washer. I put them in the washer and turned the water on. I was OK for the thirty five minute cycle. When I transferred them to the dryer, I began to wonder what I would do with them when the drying cycle was through.

There is some disagreement as to what to do with the clothes and all the other things a person leaves behind. Some people leave the deceased's room exactly the way it was, creating a shrine. Others feel that parting with everything immediately is best, that it is no longer useful, and it's only logical to get rid of it. If that is the case, I am not a logical person.

Someone suggested keeping one thing, one of Stephen's football or basketball trophies, maybe, giving it a place of honor in the living room. But Stephen was so much more than one thing. All of his stuff mattered to me. I folded the clothes and put them in his room.

There were books, notebooks, posters, cassette tapes, video tapes, pictures, and more clothes than I ever knew he owned because they had never all been in any one place at the same time. There were flattened pennies from Disneyworld, Hard Rock guitar pins, souvenirs from so many places, Nintendo games, sports magazines, Braves' paraphernalia, after shave, cologne, baseball caps, baseball cards, a world of *things*. One day it hadn't even seemed like an especially large collection of belongings, the next it was overwhelming. I knew that keeping a shrine for twenty years wouldn't be healthy, but I wasn't sure at this point in time that I could avoid it.

Parting with anything seemed like a betrayal. It was like pretending he never existed somehow. The magnets on the refrigerator, boasting of the vacations we had shared, stabbed me each time I looked at them, but I refused to take them down.

Someone, meaning well, but alarming me beyond belief, told me that as Stephen's memory faded from me, it would be easier to part with his things. I went into an all out panic. I would never forfeit his memory in exchange for the pain. I would rather hurt forever than to forget anything.

A few weeks after Stephen died, Isabelle left for Paris. She had planned to spend her summer here in Atlanta, but the tragedy had changed her plans. She needed the comfort of home. I had her over the night before she left and she asked me in a kind and apprehensive voice if she could take something of Stephen's with her. She gave me a way to avoid creating the shrine.

She took a tee shirt, one of his favorites, and she kept it with her in the cabin of the plane, so that if her luggage were lost, the shirt wouldn't be. What better way for me to part with it? It meant something to her, she cared about him, and she treasured the shirt. The first letter I received from her told me that she sometimes slept in the shirt and she dreamed of him when she slept in it.

I gave more stuff away. I was fortunate that Rick, Stephanie's husband, wore the same size clothes as Stephen. A lot of Stephen's things were new and it only made sense that someone should be wearing them. Other tee shirts and pants were taken and treasured by other friends, certain other objects from his room as well.

Of course, I kept plenty and I didn't care what anyone said about it. I put his towels in with mine and always used them when I took a shower. Seeing his towels in the wash and in the closet made me feel a little less lonely.

After a shower one morning, I removed his towel from my hair and looked in the mirror. I saw an old person. I had always wondered when it would happen, when I would start to look old. I had no idea it would happen in the matter of a few weeks. But then I didn't know I would lose a child.

A couple of weeks before Stephen died, Ron and I were going out and I was looking in a mirror, complaining about my hips. I had lost weight while my dad was sick, but my hips were still prominent.

Stephen had laughed at me. "I don't know why you always worry," he said. "You look good to be forty-one."

I had laughed, calling it a backward compliment, but I knew he meant it sincerely. In his little heart, he had thought I was as pretty as Princess Diana and as smart as Einstein. No wonder he would be impossible to replace. No one in the world, not even my daughter, thought that.

Stephanie spent a lot of time with me and we tried to keep each other sane. She, too, looked at herself in the mirror. "I look thirty," she said. "Look at the circles under my eyes."

"Look at mine."

"You got me beat, I'll admit it, but we both look horrible. You know, if Stephen were to materialize in this room right now, *he* would be the one to scream. Not us."

I had to smile at her ever present sense of humor.

"After he got through screaming, he'd say, '*My God, how long have I been dead? I thought it was only a few weeks, but from the looks of you two, it's been years,*'" she continued.

"He wouldn't want us to do this to ourselves," I said.

"Got any helpful clues on how to not do this?" she asked sarcastically.

"Not a one."

"Me, either."

Back in the mirror, it surprised me to see my reflection as whole when it really wasn't. I felt that I should have a huge gaping hole where my heart once was. I should at least have a scar somewhere or be missing a limb or two. But I looked whole.

I tried to take a deep breath, but realized that I couldn't. I realized that I hadn't taken a deep breath since he had died. It hurt to breathe. It hurt in my chest and it grabbed in my back. I had to take small shallow breaths and I tired so easily.

Going up and down the stairs exhausted me, when I had never before given it a thought. It was as if the weight of the world was on my shoulders. Grief is physically hard as well as mentally. I took naps and thought I had some dread disease and didn't care if I did.

There were so many people who never left me. Ron and Stephanie had started to construct the raft early on. Ron's two children who were now mine, added some wood by talking to me about losing their mother. They were so young when their mother died—thirteen and seven. Their bravery gave me strength. Ron's daughter, also named Kristin, had turned nine the day Stephen died. Nathan was fourteen and heartbroken at having lost the older brother he had just gained.

My aunt, one of the aunts who loved Guns N' Roses, had lost her son to cancer when he was twenty three, some twenty nine years ago. She called me often, adding wood to my raft.

My friend who had lost her brother in a car wreck added wood. When I spoke of how much I missed

Stephen, she would say very kindly and matter of factly, "You'll see him again," with a nod of her head. Even if I weren't a Christian, the conviction in her voice would have convinced me. She had said these same words to me the day he died, the day she had thrown the lifeline.

She called Stephanie and talked to her as well. Everyone told us that the pain lessened, but it never went away. I couldn't even imagine it lessening.

My two sisters and my brother brought wood for the raft. My friend, Billie Jean, brought wood. My sister Wanda, a resident of St. Simons Island now, asked me to come visit her. Billie Jean didn't want me driving it alone, so she went with me.

But just as I hadn't been aware of the lifeline being thrown at first, I wasn't aware now that a raft was being constructed. I still had no hope. I quit my job of ten years and sunk in depression.

I had never been away from Stephen for more than a week and a half in his life. I remembered how glad I was to see him after that separation. Yet here it was going on three months. Had he moved to Paris or joined the army, I still would have never been away from him this long. I would have flown to wherever he was and hugged him and kissed his face over and over, no matter how embarrassed he was. I think he would have laughed and hugged and kissed me back, especially if a lot of people weren't watching.

But I couldn't get to him. Or could I? Ron and I went on vacation in July and I stared from the moving cruise ship into the blue water. The white ship reflecting on the rippling water gave the illusion of angels moving their wings just beneath the surface and I stared, mesmerized. Were they really angels? And if I jumped, would Stephen be the one to catch me? Would he say, *Mama, I'm so glad to see you? I've never been away from you for three months.* Or would he say, *You have to go back to Stephanie, to Ron, your chores aren't through?*

Poor Stephanie, grieving so hard for the little brother she had lost. Suicide would be a selfish, horrible cowardly thing, but oh God, how could I exist for years without seeing Stephen?

I thought of my aunt once again, the one who had lost her son when he was twenty three, twenty nine long years ago. He had been gone longer than he was here. Did she remember him? Did his memory fade? Oh, God, no, don't let Stephen ever fade from my memory.

My aunt had told me to look at all the good things she had in her life. Her other children, her grandchildren, great grandchildren, nieces, nephews, sisters and brothers, so many people who loved and needed her. She told me to think about all she would have missed had she just laid down and died when her son did. Her son had died on her birthday, yet she said she had had happy birthdays and many happy times since then. She assured me that I would laugh—and live again.

I, of course, still couldn't imagine it. I *still* didn't know the raft was being constructed. Ron and I went to Chastain Park to see Ringo Starr. I tried to let the music take me back to my childhood, a time before the pain. It didn't work. The music only served as a guilty reminder that Stephen wasn't even born when I had listened to that music and he was gone and I was still here.

At forty one, I felt guilt at having lived too long a life. Forty one didn't seem that old to most people, but it was *too* old for me. If my son had only been allowed to live eighteen years, I was way overdue to die. I didn't look good to be forty one anymore. The music didn't invite dancing. Life didn't beckon the way it always had before.

By the time the evening with Ringo was drawing to a close, I was worn out from fighting the guilt. About that time, Ringo starts to sing *Photograph*. *All I have is a photograph and I know you won't be coming back anymore.* I lost it—right in the stands, causing a sixteen year old boy next to me to ask what was wrong.

I had talked casually with the teenager before the concert started and found that he appreciated old songs in the same way Stephen did. I told him now that I had lost my son in a car accident and I felt bad when I saw tears come to his eyes. He hugged me and said, *I bet you were a really cool mom.* This sixteen year old stranger added wood to the raft.

The shock was gone and the pain was raw. I was no longer allowed to leave my body in a crumpled heap by the washer and go on like a zombie. My body demanded to be healed, the issue demanded to be addressed and I didn't know how.

I would be eating lunch or driving down the road and without warning, an overwhelming sense of loss would hit my body. It was almost like a cruel voice inside my head would say, *Stephen is dead* and it would seem as if I had heard the news of his death for the very first time. I would throw the lunch away or I would burst into tears as I drove. *You have lost this precious child—how can you go on?* the cruel voice would demand. I would be devastated anew—it would shock my system each time.

In conversation, someone would refer to *at Stephen's funeral* and it would hit me like a lightning bolt, reinforcing to me that he was dead, gone from me. The cruel voice would ask, *How are you living day to day? How dare you drive down the road like a normal human being, how dare you eat, breathe and sleep.*

Don't get me wrong. It wasn't that I hadn't hurt at the very beginning. I had. My heart had hurt, I had been to Stephen's room and cried, holding his big shirt and his little baby blanket and buried my face in the pillowcase that still smelled like him.

But the anesthesia would kick in and the broken body would get up and walk away, tired, exhausted, zombie like. My body would shut down and I would go to sleep. I suppose one would die without the anesthesia called shock in the beginning. They couldn't cope with the loss.

But now the safety valve was off and I had to find a way to live with this. The anesthesia can't last forever and the pain is devastating when it leaves, there's no escape. At the beginning I had told myself I *had* to handle this, I had no choice, it was final. Of course, the shock was playing a bigger part than I knew. Now I asked *why* should I have to handle this, *why* did it have to happen, *why* did he have to die?

The pain was so bad, I decided the only way to live was to deny the pain. I was OK, I told myself over and over. I told my friends the same thing, I told my family. They all marveled at how strong I was. This was working, I told myself, but then I joined a grief group and they saw through my lie.

They knew all about denial, something I thought I had invented. They encouraged grief, they encouraged leaning into the pain. I didn't like that idea. They also said anger was a part of grieving. I didn't like that, either. They said you could be angry at others, yourself, the person who died, they even said it was OK to be mad at God, that He was a big guy and He could take it. Wasn't that sacrilegious? I wasn't mad at myself, I wasn't mad at God, I certainly wasn't mad at Stephen, I wasn't mad at anybody.

CHAPTER EIGHT

Anger & Guilt

OK, so maybe I was mad at those people who had acted the way they did over the music at the funeral. OK, I'll admit that. And I was mad at them because they didn't realize how important it was to honor what Stephen would have wanted. And because they didn't think it was important to honor what Stephen would have wanted *must* mean that they didn't know how important Stephen was. They must not have known his significance.

My child hadn't lived to reach adulthood and I needed to prove his significance because he hadn't had a chance to make his own way. He was just beginning, he didn't have a chance to prove himself. It was obvious no one had a clue of just how valuable the child was.

I was sure that he had a very promising life ahead of him. I knew how successful he would have been, how good he would have turned out. I knew because of the way he always took the good with the bad and went right on smiling. Apparently, only I knew what a wonderful person he was and would have been. To most everyone else, he was nothing more than a reckless teenager.

So it began. Anger. Anger that people didn't realize Stephen's significance in the world, in my life, his significance, period. This anger grew to an all consuming hate that no one had loved him like I did, like they should have. But no one loves a child like a mother does, no one—how could I expect them to feel what I did? Before my dance with anger was over, I was angry at myself, God, and most everybody who drew breath on a regular basis.

I was putting new flowers at the tree Stephen had hit and a red sports car stopped. The driver was a twenty-something very tanned muscular male. "Was it your son?" he asked and I nodded. "I heard it was a teenager," he shrugged.

Shrugging is OK when you talk about it raining on a day you had planned to go to the beach or even if your favorite football team just got shut out by their worst rival, but not when you're talking about someone's son dying.

"It's a bad curve," the tanned man continued casually. "He probably wasn't paying attention."

OK. I had reached a point in my life where I either needed to become deaf or get a gun. I was still debating on which one when he added more. "You know, when I was eighteen, I was frustrated and confused. He's probably better off." The gun it would be.

But for now, I didn't have one. "For your information, we think he swerved to miss someone walking in the road," I said. "I think he gave his life to save someone else. And even if he didn't, even if he wasn't *paying attention*, do you think he deserved to die? Don't shrug my son off—don't you ever shrug my son off!"

The muscular man knew he was in deep.

"As for your frustration theory, we all get frustrated, just ask me—I'm the queen of it right now, buddy, and I don't want to die. *I don't want to die*," I repeated quietly for my own benefit, realizing that I didn't want to die. "I don't want to die," I said again.

He left fast, thinking I was crazier than I really was, which was pretty bad, considering. I wasn't sure if I should chase him down and thank him or proceed with buying the gun. Probably the latter.

"I don't want to die," I said again and again, amazed.

Then I kicked the tree so hard it shook and went on my way.

I didn't want to die, but I was still very unhappy that Stephen had. Before Stephen died, cemeteries gave me the creeps. I would have never dreamed of being there at twilight, much less after dark. But now, to be there at midnight on a foggy night was in no way frightening. I walked up to the mausoleum and I stood beside it, staring at his picture that was placed on the wall.

It wasn't the first time I had made the midnight trip, but it was the first time it had been cold. I stood in the darkness, shivering. It was September and it was going to get much colder. The cruel uninvited thought came to me that Stephen was inside this building and it was cold. I had tried to make sure that little body was protected from heat and cold all his life and now—now I couldn't. I had had the same horrible thought when the summer sun beat down on it.

I knew the approaching car lights were Ron's and I turned to face him. He was probably thanking God for small favors that I wasn't lying against the wall, screaming, as he had found me many times before. I told him what I was thinking.

He reminded me gently that the mausoleum would be enclosed soon, that Stephen would be inside, that was the reason we had bought the crypt we did. If Ron had a dime for every time he's said to me, "'It's just his body, honey—his soul is in heaven,'" he'd be a rich man. He said it again.

But I loved that little body that had housed that soul. I loved it so much. I told Ron I was OK and that I would be home in a little while. He reluctantly left and I laid my head against the cold wall and cried.

What had I done to deserve this? It had to be pretty bad. There were mass murderers and all kinds of horrible people on this Earth who had never lost a child. One might think that I would have figured out at this point that I wasn't being punished, but I simply concluded that these murderers and criminals must have some redeeming quality that I didn't have.

Oh, my God—maybe that guy who said that God took Stephen because I got a divorce was right. Horror ran through my veins. If I had stayed with someone who was abusing me mentally and physically, would Stephen still be here? I would have stayed. I would have taken it.

I knew people who had stayed in horrible marriages because they didn't believe in divorce, people with six and eight children and all of those children were still alive. What were the odds? I had given birth to two and had lost one. It was my fault, it really was. It was my fault for not staying in a bad situation.

This made me angry at myself and with God. What a stupid rule. I did the unthinkable—I finally screamed at God. "So all the teenagers with two parents get to live—isn't that just great? Stephen had a harder life than those kids because he didn't have two parents and a safe little family life—and yet you think he wasn't as good as all of them?" I screamed at the top of my lungs.

"Is that why you took him? We tried our best, he had to try harder than the other kids and then you take him because I divorced a man who hit me? You want to know what I think of that?" I know for a fact there is no such thing as screaming loudly enough to wake the dead because I would have had a lot of company.

My voice was hoarse and leaving me and I knew it, but I still hurled one final question. "You didn't love him like I did either, did you?" I screamed accusingly and sunk to the ground, crying.

Stephen is on the second row of the mausoleum and when I sunk to the ground, I was leaning back against an empty crypt. I remembered the night when I had watched the scary movie sitting on the floor and Stephen was on the sofa above me and I found comfort. I sat there a long time with him just above me.

I awoke the next morning with no voice, but plenty of thoughts running through my head. I turned the TV on for a distraction. A preacher was giving an inspirational thought for the day. He spoke of sunshine, flowers and rain. He was stressing that rain came to all of us and that flowers couldn't grow without rain and sunshine. I got his point, but I didn't feel a lot like a flower and I didn't see how Stephen's death could possibly make me grow.

Besides, if God had taken Stephen from me because I hadn't been a good person and He was punishing me, He wouldn't call me His flower. Or maybe He would call me His flower, but He certainly wouldn't care if I had sunshine or rain or was yanked out of the ground by heavy winds and blown to oblivion.

When you start thinking this way, there is no relief, no good can come of it. I remembered hearing a story at church a few years ago, the story of a father and son camping. It's dark and the little boy is scared. He's afraid that he and his dad are lost, though he doesn't want his dad to know he thinks that. He's afraid he'll never see his mother again. He's afraid of all the noises he's hearing. He doesn't say anything, but his dad answers anyway.

"I know where we are," the dad says. "I know where you want to be. I know how to get you there." What a comfort that must have been to the child. The point, of course, was that our Heavenly Father knows where we are, He knows where we need to be and He knows how to get us there. Well—I hoped so, I thought skeptically.

I had gone to a small chapel in the upstairs of my large liberal church the Sunday after Stephen's funeral and had very honestly told God that I didn't know how to deal with this and would He please help me?

I had felt that He would, but since my midnight massacre of myself at the mausoleum, doubt had completely taken over.

That night, my throat still scratchy, I lay in bed very near sleep. Sometimes I think God is closest to us when we are sleeping or very near sleep. I thought of a sweet couple, married most of their lives, who had placed their forty four year old daughter in the same mausoleum just three weeks after Stephen had died. She had been shot in the head by her husband. The father had found her. Those parents had done nothing to deserve losing a child or finding her in such a horrible way.

In the same mausoleum was a nineteen month old baby boy named Spencer. He had died in 1995. His parents were still together. The mother was pregnant with the second child when Spencer died. They were now expecting their third child. They had done nothing to deserve losing a child. *I* had done nothing to deserve losing a child. I finally realized there was nothing a human being could do that was bad enough to deserve a punishment so severe as losing a child. Nothing.

I felt that these thoughts were sent to me directly by a messenger of God and I was very surprised that He was still speaking to me. *What were you thinking?* the voice asked. *There are plenty of people in this world who have several children and lose one or more when they aren't divorced, sometimes people with only one child lose that child when they aren't divorced. Then there are people who are divorced or never married and never lose a child.*

Could God really be sending me these thoughts? Did He love me after all, even though I had yelled at Him?

The thought that followed was another unsolicited one. *What if the tables were turned, what if you were the one inside that mausoleum and Stephen was the one outside, screaming at midnight, unable to cope? Had you been the one to die, you would have wanted him to go on, to be strong.*

The horrible thought hit me that Stephen could see me. It would hurt him so badly to see me hurting this way. I had to do better.

I had to quit paying attention to every stupid thing people said about divorce and everything else. I had to grieve the right way and I had to trust God. I couldn't see His face in the windshield, but maybe I would see it in the rear view mirror. Maybe someday I would understand. This was our current pastor's favorite saying. He said if you couldn't see God's hand, you had to trust His heart and he said it was a good heart. I had to trust that.

It rains on the just and unjust and *bad things happen to good people* seem like such *sayings*, but they aren't just *sayings*.

They have to be taken to heart. The way one deals with the rain and the bad things that are thrown our way are a test of character. It makes you who you are. And I decided that I wouldn't be defeated. I wouldn't lay down and die. I would run the race that was set before me with perseverance, as the Bible says. By God, I would make it through this.

I awoke with a purpose in my life. I had to tell Stephen I was OK. I was bustling around the house, thinking of books I had read that said spirits existed right beside us, though we couldn't see them. What if Stephen had been right beside me and tried to comfort me all along and I couldn't hear him? That would be so horrible for him. I had to go to the cemetery. Not that he was really there, but I felt I could talk to him there.

I walked with determination down the hall and Ron stepped out of the kitchen just as I reached it. I walked right into him, hitting my bare toe against his hard shoe, breaking my little toe. After howling in pain and cursing my clumsiness, I headed for the cemetery to tell Stephen of my new resolution. The thought of him worrying about me had left a powerful imprint on my mind.

I limped up to the mausoleum wall. "Don't worry about the limp," I said immediately. "I'm OK. I just broke my toe. I walked into Ron. You know how he's always right under me."

Maybe I'm really crazy, but I swear I heard Stephen laugh. His laughter was inside my head as the thoughts from the night before had been, but it was very real. And I knew why he was laughing.

I had told him many times that if and when I married again, it would have to be to a man who traveled a lot, because I would feel smothered after having been divorced for so long. Ron was the exact opposite of what I thought I would marry and Stephanie and Stephen found it comical to have their mother in such a close marriage.

I heard him laugh again, as if he had thought about it and had to let out another laugh. "I'm going to do better with this grieving thing, Stephen. I miss you so much, but I'll do better. For you."

Even though this was substantial progress, a milestone, it was far from over. Guilt and anger crept back in time and again, sometimes as a pair, sometimes individually, but never again with the force of that night at the mausoleum.

There is a picture on my bedroom wall of a mother and a child. I bought it when Stephen was two or three. A friend of mine was having a home decorating party and I called to tell her I had too much to do at home, that I couldn't make the party. She said that I must come, that there was a picture that looked just like Stephen and me. I laughed and told her she'd do anything to make a sale.

I went to the party and when I saw the picture, I was amazed. It truly did look like Stephen and me. I bought it on the spot. It graced our living room wall for years, then in later years, I moved it to my bedroom. Stephen would look at the picture and sometimes smile, remembering when it had looked like the two of us.

I immediately hung the picture in my and Ron's bedroom when we got married. Stephen was in the bedroom the night before he died, talking to me about his tax refund and his plans for spending it the next day. I saw him glance at the picture and smile, obviously glad that it still hung in my bedroom in the house that was still unfamiliar to both of us.

The picture had always been a source of joy for me, but the night he died and thereafter, it was not. The picture is a young mother with long hair, holding a little boy with thick blonde hair, just like Stephen had at that age. The mother's arms are securely around him, he is resting safely against her.

I felt as responsible for him at eighteen as I had when I bought the picture. I had failed him, I hadn't protected him. The picture now haunted me each night as I went to sleep.

Guilt and anger would drop in unexpectedly in the daytime in the form of a *Star Wars* commercial. The year Stephen died was also the twentieth anniversary of the movie and a comeback was in full swing. Stephen wasn't even born when the movie had come out, but he had caught it on the second go round and had been around for *The Empire Strikes Back* and *Return of the Jedi*.

A pain stabbed deep in my heart as I watched the creatures on the TV screen, remembering the action figures from these movies that had called our place home. The figures had gone on vacation with us, and graced every room of our house, Stephen usually lying on his stomach, intently positioning them.

He wasn't even born when Star Wars came out and you were twenty two, the now familiar guilt stabbed. It wasn't fair. I should be the one gone, not him.

Watching football was bittersweet. I no longer had all the inside info from Stephen. I watched blindly, but I watched—especially the Raiders. I remembered the shirts, the caps, the bandanas.

Stephen had the usual fantasies of playing pro as a child. He ran around the house and yard, playing both offense and defense and announcing as he played. It was quite a talent.

I took one of the Raider bandanas from his room to the mausoleum, tying it onto the flower vase. I had always known that his chances of playing for the Raiders, as he always pretended, were slim to none, but I had never *ever* dreamed that I would take one of those bandanas and hang it on a mausoleum wall. He should be here, watching the football games, not me.

Remembering all the times we had shared, I began to feel that nothing could come close to what Stephen and I had had. No one could come close to being Stephen. I began to saint him and leave everyone else in the cold.

CHAPTER NINE

Minimizing the Loss

*J*ust as I began to saint Stephen, it seemed that everyone else was minimizing my loss. These two did not go well together. I searched for comfort and came up short. Anger still visited a lot, a more frequent visitor than guilt now.

I had promised to not pay attention to stupid things people said, but it was easier said than done. I ran into an acquaintance of Stephanie's and mine and I asked if she had seen Stephanie lately. She said *yes*. I said, "I guess she told you about Stephen," and she said *yes* and frowned. "But that's been months," she shrugged. "The two of you should be doing better by now."

Excuse me. Just as I had been infuriated at the muscular man at the tree with that shrug and those minimizing words, it came back again. Shrugging is not good. It minimizes. Many things spoken minimize. Minimizing is not good. How hard is it to say, "He was a wonderful child. You must miss him horribly"?

A few weeks later, I ran into an older acquaintance in a shopping center. I debated on whether to bring it up or not. I had a feeling she knew, but what if she didn't? Months later when I happened to run into her again, would she say *I can't believe you didn't tell me?* So I asked, "Did you hear about Stephen?"

She nodded and shrugged. "Nothing I can say. These things happen."

I realize she didn't know what to say and she wished I wouldn't have brought it up. But once again, *I'm so sorry* would have been better. That shrug and those words minimized the loss and made me furious. I didn't say anything but I wanted to scream, "You still have your two children, don't you? They're older than I am. If one of them were to die, would you shrug and say *these things happen?* I highly doubt it."

I kept so much inside me, it's a miracle I didn't literally explode. But if I had jumped everyone's case that ticked me off, someone would have surely put me in the looney bin because I would have been raving constantly.

Many people never said a word. Most of the neighbors on our street acted as though nothing had happened. I know some people have a harder time than others saying something, but silence minimizes, like losing Stephen wasn't worth mentioning.

I realize that some of them, when they saw me again, didn't want to bring it up. Maybe I had a smile on my face and they thought I would burst into tears at the mention of it. It's never too late to say you're sorry and the person you're saying it to has in no way, not for a second, forgotten the loss. They smile, they function, but it has never left their mind. Even in their sleep, they never forget. "I was sorry to hear about your son," were welcome words. Silence was taken as minimizing.

On the other side of the coin, you have the friends who did take it hard, who felt your loss so deeply that they can't understand how you can live without this child. They almost make you feel guilty for smiling or joking or laughing again. They tell you repeatedly that they couldn't do it, that they would just die if they lost their child, they would never laugh or talk or joke again. They would be forever devastated. They don't know *how* they would be. They haven't been where you are.

They say they can't believe you didn't have a nervous breakdown, almost as if that is what they expect of you. I even had a couple of friends tell me that they thought they were taking Stephen's death as hard as I was, that maybe they were hurting *more*. They said this because they didn't see me grieving the way they *thought* I should grieve.

Grieve for yourself, grieve for the one you lost in the way that works for you. Try to ignore these people who think you should be screaming from daylight to dark, do not try to grieve the way they think you should. Do not feel guilty that you didn't have a nervous breakdown or that you aren't screaming from sunup to sundown. Thank God that you aren't.

These same people who claim to be taking things harder than you are the very ones who will ask months later how *long* it has been since the death. Seems that they would remember the date, seeing as how they were grieving as much as you, but they don't.

You, of course, could tell them to the hour how long it has been, but you'll just say the horrible date, and they'll say casually, *Really? I thought it had been longer* or *I didn't realize it had been that long.* Then they will once again tell you that they think they took it as hard as you did. I think not.

Because these people are friends and closer to you, it's a little easier to tell them to shut up, but at first you take it badly. You think *I've been trying so hard to come out of this and live and now I'm being condemned for surviving.*

Then you realize you are the one in this up to your neck, they aren't. You live with it day in and day out, they don't. Their lives go on, it's on your mind every minute and you have to find a way to deal with it in order to survive. As time goes on, even to the best of your friends, it will become one of those horrible things that happened. To you, it is a wound that you have successfully stopped the bleeding of or you wouldn't have lived. They'll think about the death with sadness, but they weren't bleeding to death as you were.

I worked in a very large dental practice at the time of Stephen's death. I had worked in this practice since Stephen was eight years old. Some of the patients felt that they knew Stephen, even though they had never met him. Many of them had met him. They had been in the office when Stephen was there for a cleaning or had dropped by to get money, one of his favorite pastimes as he got older.

I was out for two weeks after Stephen's death and by the time I returned, many of the patients knew. I saw many grown men with tears in their eyes. Others called on the phone and choked on their tears as they tried to tell me how sorry they were. One openly sobbed. Women came in and hugged me without saying a word, one brought flowers from her garden. They didn't have appointments, they just came. This meant a lot. It meant they cared. It meant they knew the loss was huge. It wasn't minimal. They felt the pain.

This is the job I quit shortly after Stephen died. Cards and letters filled my mailbox like Christmas cards for months as other caring patients found out about Stephen when they went for their check-ups. They told me that they thought of me often, that they thought of Stephen. The loss wasn't minimized. I found comfort in that.

There was comfort in people saying nice things about Stephen. Feeling that he would always be remembered was a comfort. A wonderful child, a fun loving teen-ager, a man in so many ways was on this earth for eighteen years, eight months and twenty some odd days and I didn't want it to ever be forgotten. When I began to realize that a lot of people felt this way, I began to heal.

My eight year old nephew, Alex, who always thought Stephen was *cool*, had watched Stephen's every move and mimicked his way of walking and talking long before Stephen died. When Alex goes across the yard, purposefully walking that way, I know Stephen is remembered.

Alex's fourteen year old brother, Adam, laughs at things Stephen did and his eyes smile like Stephen's. He, too, can mimic Stephen perfectly. He has the shoulder movement down and will say, *What's happening, dude?* very much like Stephen. I find comfort in knowing that they looked up to him and loved him enough to copy him.

Lauren and Brittany, Stephanie's four year old twins, tell me that their Uncle 'tephen is safe in their hearts. They draw pictures for him and stick them in his flowers at the mausoleum.

Stephen's friends have been a huge source of comfort. They truly cared for him. They have helped more than they will ever know to establish his significance, his worth, his value. He was significant to them. The loss was never minimized, not for a second with them.

In November, as rain poured outside my window, I sadly watched. This was my first November without Stephen since I was twenty two years old. I took a small plastic container from our art supplies and walked out onto the deck. I held it out to the rain. It filled quickly and I snapped the top on, found a string and tied it to the container.

The phone rang and it was a friend of his, saying she was on her way to the cemetery. I told her I was, as well, with November rain in a plastic container. She gasped, saying what a great idea it was and she arrived with her own vial of November rain. Day by day, the containers multiplied. Isabelle even sent November rain from Paris.

The next month, Isabelle returned from Paris to spend Christmas with me, easing me through what could have been a horrible holiday. We shopped and she told me funny things Stephen had done and I showed her baby pictures of him and we made cheesecake. She truly warmed my Christmas.

Kristin, though she never met Stephen in the physical world, but held him in her arms just as he had slipped from his body, constantly lets me know that he is significant to her. She said he changed her life in a drastic way for the better. She visits me and asks to see pictures of him and movies.

Sheree, the friend who met me at the cemetery with November rain, was a long time friend of Stephen's. They had dated for a short time and had remained friends forever. Sheree was now married to Johnny, another long time friend of Stephen's. Both of them stuck close by my side during the holidays. I gave them Christmas gifts and felt less lonely, then we went out for pizza, Stephen's favorite food.

Johnny and Stephen's voices were always so similar, it was hard to tell them apart on the phone. They had spent many years tricking Sheree, calling her house and saying it was one when it was the other. It kept her life interesting, to say the least.

Sometimes Johnny would call the house and when he would say hello, I would think it was Stephen, even though Stephen would be standing in front of me. I had often wondered why their voices were so much alike. Now I think it's God's little favor to me.

Johnny is a very quiet person, but doesn't mind that I'm always asking him to talk. When I'm on the phone with

Sheree, he'll always take the phone and say a few words because he knows I love hearing his voice. I also know how much he loved Stephen and that means just as much to me.

As 1997 drew to a close, I was convinced that God had left me here for a reason, my chores weren't done. I would survive and I would be proud to have survived after being dealt such a cruel blow. I would help other people who suffer loss. My raft was built. Maybe I could help build that raft for someone else. Unfortunately, I wouldn't be the last person on Earth to lose a child.

In January, I saw an old flicker of me in the mirror. Maybe some hope in my eyes. I was surprised and stared, but it disappeared again quickly. But—at least I knew it was still there. My brother asked me to come help him with paperwork in his cabinet shop. He needed me and I desperately needed to be needed. Being with him has helped me to redistribute the weight.

Redistributing the Weight

My dad had a stroke in March of 1996. He fought it a year. Before the battle was over in March of 1997, he was a quadriplegic with a stomach tube. It was no way to live. I will always believe Stephen and my dad were soul mates, happy to be reunited in Heaven after only an earthly month's separation.

I had never seen Stephen cry so hard as the day my dad's stroke came or the day my dad died. Neither Stephen nor I slept much while Daddy was in the funeral home. Stephen lay on the sofa in the living room, talking about his Daddy Ralph and I leaned back in the recliner all night, both nights. To date, it was the worst thing that had ever happened to us.

When Stephen was small and a little unhappy that I had taken his bottle away, Daddy appeared with a coffee mug with a sipper top. Stephen never gave the bottle another thought, he had a cup like Daddy Ralph's. Stephen smiled as we talked about it.

Stephen's black lab had rapidly outgrown our apartment and had lived most of his life in my parents' backyard.

Some of Stephen's happiest moments were spent in that back yard with my dad and that dog. Sometimes I imagine them in Heaven, throwing a stick to that wonderful dog and laughing. I know there's no Biblical evidence that pets go to Heaven, but I can't imagine a perfect place without them. I think Spook, Stephen's black cat, is there also. I think Stephen walks around holding that cat and stroking her head the way he did here.

I see Heaven as a very physical place with lakes and streams and mountains to climb. I see it as just like here, only better. And I know that Daddy and Stephen are there, together once again.

Daddy died on March 11th and I grieved for a month and two days. Stephen died on April 13th. I was crying the night before Stephen died. I told him that I missed my dad. He hugged me, then asked me if I was sure nothing else was wrong. He had a hard time trusting men after what the two of us had been through.

I assured him nothing else was wrong and he sat down on my bed and talked for a while. It was a Friday night and things being what they were, Stephen had things to do and people to see and he went on his way before long. It wasn't the last time I saw him, but it was just over twenty four hours before he died. My heart was yanked from my body and I could no longer grieve for my dad.

This troubled me to no end. I had loved my daddy dearly. It was one of the first things I told the grief counselor. He was very sympathetic.

"One expects to say goodbye at some point in time to parents," he said kindly. "We know from the minute we're old enough to think rationally that if all goes well and everybody lives healthy lives, the parents will get old and the children will have to let them go. It's been in the back of our minds all our lives. It's still sad, but our mind is somewhat conditioned. The mind can never be conditioned to losing a child. A child dying before a parent leaves a horrible wound. And then, there's the matter of significance."

Significance. There was that word again.

"With a child, it's a matter of hanging on, instead of letting go. You need people to know how wonderful this child *would have* been. Your dad left his mark. Stephen didn't have a chance to."

My dad, had indeed, left his mark. Maybe not on the world, but certainly on his family. He had four children and grandchildren who would make sure his memory lived on. He had taught all of us so much, even when he didn't know he was teaching.

When I was fifteen, I was holding my brother Phil, five years old at the time, up to the window, watching Daddy cut grass on a riding lawnmower. It was 1971 and the lawnmower was a new item at our house and we were rather impressed. My two sisters also watched. The lawnmower was second hand and the engine was skipping. We knew Daddy would work on it for hours after he was through with the grass.

Meanwhile, he was clowning a little and we were laughing. He went up a hill and the lawnmower skipped roughly, causing the lawnmower to buck, throwing him off the back. We laughed, but then the lawnmower began to roll backward toward him. He put his foot up to stop the mower and I thought all was well. What I didn't see was that his foot had slipped off the body of the mower and had gone underneath into the blade.

My sister Wanda ran out the door, looking alarmed. I followed and saw him walking up the hill, his shoe torn to shreds, his big toe hanging by a piece of skin, his foot mangled. "Get your mother," he said calmly. "Get your mother." He was in shock. He wasn't hurting. It must have been fifteen minutes or more before he felt the pain. We were halfway to the hospital and he bit his lip. He lost the big toe and half of the second one and had a nasty gash along the bone.

It hurt for months. It hurt a lot. He said the pain became a dull ache after a while. Just when we would think it was healing, an infection would invade. He had to learn to walk without the big toe for balance. It would be his new sense of normal. He said he could do it, that he didn't have a choice, that he had to learn to *redistribute the weight*, but the first time it snowed, he fell several times.

Ten years later, during a visit to my parents', Daddy came walking through the house without a shoe, which wasn't unusual for him by then, but because he didn't have a sock on as he usually did, Stephanie and Stephen started asking him questions about his missing toe. I was amazed that he walked perfectly, his balance totally restored. I told him as much.

He said, "I'm always aware that it's gone. At first, I couldn't walk without my shoe, obviously now I can. It doesn't get infected anymore and it doesn't hurt like it did, but I'm always aware that it's gone. Sometimes," he said slowly, "it's the weirdest thing, but I still feel it as if it's right there."

I thought of him now. I was in shock when Stephen died, then just when I thought I was healing, I would have a major relapse. I said I could live with the tragedy, I didn't have a choice, but I fell a lot learning to live without Stephen. I'm always aware that Stephen's gone from me, even in my sleep. It doesn't hurt as excruciatingly as it did at first, the pain has become a dull ache. It's my new sense of normal. And sometimes, it still feels as if Stephen's right there beside me.

Daddy taught me things when he didn't even know he was.

One night, after meeting other parents who had lost children at the cemetery, a friend who was with me remarked, "You know, without a question, you're all survivors and should be proud of it, but there's an identical look of brokeness on each of your faces."

That's because a piece of our heart is missing. It's hard for it not to show. It was a piece that was allotted only for Stephen, only for these people's sons and daughters in their hearts. Maybe we had all found a new sense of normal that we could live with, but our lives have been forever changed. And though no one can fill the spot that

Stephen left in my heart, I will take the hands of those who are so willing to help me redistribute the weight.

Less than a week after Stephen died, Ron and I were sitting in a sandwich shop with Lauren and Brittany. I was completely lost in thought—thoughts of how in the world I was going to live through this. Lauren was calling my name over and over. Finally, she knocked on my head and said, "Knock, knock is anybody in there? I need to talk you something."

And so it was—a lot of people needed to *talk me something*, and I decided to listen. They needed me in their lives and they saved mine.

When you almost die, you appreciate life more. I love my daughter like I never did before and believe me, I already loved her a lot. She was born when I was sixteen and we grew up together. She has been like my right arm all along. She kept Stephen after school while I worked from the time she was twelve years old. She helped me with everything. She was no different in his death.

Devastated herself, she rallied herself together for me. Mother's Day came just a few weeks after Stephen died and she gave me a card telling me what she and Stephen had always liked best about me and assured me that they would both love me forever. She also assured me that if anything happened to me, she would be a twenty five year old orphan and told me that I couldn't let that happen.

I also realized very quickly how much my brother and my two sisters love me. I am the oldest, but they have all taken me under their wing. Wanda's house on St. Simons rapidly became a retreat. She has the same mischievous roll of her eyes and raising of her eyebrows, the same devilish smile she had as a child. She makes me smile.

She is also an avid photographer and she pulled out tons of pictures of Stephen and stressed to me how he was always smiling, assuring me that he had had a very happy life in spite of the failed marriage and less than perfect circumstances.

The serenity prayer hung on her wall and I read it over and over. *Please, God, help me to accept the things I cannot change.* That was my plea as we walked along the beach and fed the seagulls, one of Stephen's favorite things to do.

My other sister Janet, Adam and Alex's mother, shuddered dreadfully at the loss, and though she fully understood my wanting to jump off the cruise ship the summer before, she sincerely told me that I was very needed here. She encouraged me to go on and helped me in so many ways. She was always a phone call away and she visited often.

I had all but lost touch with my brother because he was busy and I was busy. He has made it very clear that he needs me here. He needs me to keep the paperwork of his business straight as much as he needed me to watch him jump garbage cans on his Evel Knievel bike when he was a kid.

I smile as I think of our lives together—the Ricky Nelson and Richard Chamberlain marriages, Phil's stitches in his chin after an unsuccessful Evel Knievel stunt, Janet's love of Barry Manilow. As far as I know, she never pretended to marry him, but she had a life size poster in her room. It startled me many times.

And then, there was the real stuff—real weddings where we were each other's bridesmaids and ring bearers and flower girls. And real babies. I remember the day Adam was born like it was yesterday. I left the hospital and went straight to the store to buy a card that said *nephew*. I remember the Friday I left work early to go to the hospital to wait for Alex to get here. And then there was that Monday night at the hospital, waiting for Phil's little girl, Haley. And last and least, at the moment, there's Phil's little boy, Austin, an adorable two-year-old. I know a lot of people leave town during the holidays after they lose a child, but I stay home. I still have a lot to be home for.

My first maternal bond was with Phil, long before Stephen was born, and some of it has transferred back. Redistributed. His smile is the same smile he had when he was three years old, a smile that is dear to my heart. Working with him and seeing his business prosper, I *tell* him how proud I am of him. I tell him I love him. These things might never have happened had I not suffered the loss I did.

I'm sure Stephen would have turned out very much like Phil. All grown up and responsible, but never above having a whole lot of fun. I also know that if Stephen had the choice, he would ask that I stay here. He's fine now and he knows that I'll be there soon enough. Time goes by very fast in Heaven, I'm sure. He would want me here with these people who, by needing me, have helped me redistribute the weight.

CHAPTER ELEVEN

Deciding To Live

 I ran into Stephen's friends many times at the cemetery. Sometimes the visits were planned, sometimes
we just happened up there at the same time. One day one
of the girls told me of another teenage boy who had died
in a car accident a couple of years before Stephen. She
told me that a few months after he died, when she went to
visit his grave, she was surprised to find that his mother
was buried beside him.

I gasped. She told me she had worried a lot about me in
the beginning, that she didn't want to tell me this story
earlier. Had she told me earlier, I would have envied the
mother. Hearing it months later, I didn't respect it. The
woman had taken her own life, leaving other heartbroken
children behind, wondering why they hadn't been enough
to keep her here. *Didn't she love them, too?* they had asked
their father. Tears filled my eyes at the thought of all the
pain a suicide brings.

There were times just after Stephen died when I felt
that he needed me in Heaven and it drove me crazy.
Maybe this woman felt the same way. I suppose it was a

conceited thought, considering Heaven has much higher beings than myself and more comfort to offer than I ever could.

I know for a fact now that Stephen is on a higher plane and much wiser. He exists in a perfect world where one has the so called *big picture*. He understands why things happened the way they did, he understands why he was called away from us.

Had I died, too, and left Stephanie here in an imperfect world without the big picture, it would have been worse. There are things she might need that I can help her with; I am certain Stephen needs nothing where he is. I also realize that if I died, I would miss Stephanie the way I miss Stephen now, big picture or not.

I also know that Stephen would tell me that after waiting all these years to remarry, the least I can do is to want to stay here with Ron, the kind of man I didn't believe existed. Stephen knows it will be good for my soul to experience the kind of love Ron can give me, even though I have to accept it while missing him.

Stephen would also tell me that Nathan and Kristin don't need to lose another mother and he would remind me that I have a very valid place in Lauren and Brittany's hearts. He would jokingly say that Lauren and Brittany need a break from Stephanie now and then and vice versa and that I am the one who can provide that break, keeping the three of them sane. He would want me to silently look out for their dad, Rick, his brother in law and his hero, from the time he was ten years old.

He would also want me to help other people who have lost children. Stephen always expected me to fix things. In my quest to give him security as a child, I had convinced him I could fix most anything. But this was a tough assignment.

I ran into many distraught parents at the cemetery; we often shared our pain. I arrived at the cemetery one day, just at dusk, and a man stood beside the crypt of a three year old, tears falling.

He turned toward me. "She stopped breathing when she was born," he said. "I often wonder why she didn't just die then. Sometimes I wish she would have, the pain might be less."

I knew the child had died with meningitis. I knew it had to be horrible, watching helplessly as the doctors tried to save her. I grasped for words. "But you would have never had the privilege of *knowing* her. You would have missed three years of *The Dance*," I smiled to the stranger.

He nodded through his tears. "Garth Brooks," he smiled. "And you're right, of course. But it just hurts so bad."

"I know," I said truthfully.

"Who?" he asked, motioning toward the crypts.

"Stephen," I said, knowing last names weren't necessary, we were all familiar with the names, especially the children.

He cringed and fresh tears came. "Car wreck, I heard," he said and I nodded. He hugged me and left.

I sat down on the concrete below Stephen's vault and looked out across the green fields and valleys. Fields and valleys that had once swarmed with blue and gray jackets, guns and bayonets.

Cheatham's Earthworks is a half mile east of the cemetery. The cannons are still there and miles of trenches where the Confederates, under the direction of General Benjamin Cheatham, dug in deep and ambushed the Yankees. Thousands of soldiers had died. Misery was nothing new to this stretch of land. Tragedy had made its home here long before we brought our children.

Many parents had lost their sons in these fields, far away from home. Three thousand Union soldiers died, one thousand Confederates. Parents in the North saw their sons march off to battle and never laid eyes on them again.

One Confederate soldier's remains were found in the 1970's, just across the street from the cemetery, the soldier's mother's search for him still echoing from *her* grave. The soldier's remains were taken and ceremoniously laid to rest beside her.

That would be worse than the way I lost Stephen, I thought sadly. At first, I guess I felt that nothing could be worse than what had happened to Stephen and I thought that no matter how a person died, the end result was the same, dead was dead. But it could have been worse. Knowing your child died on a battlefield a thousand miles away from you, but not knowing whether he had suffered tremendously and never being able to even see the body would be worse than what I had suffered.

A car turning in the cemetery brought me back to present day. I turned and watched a man get out of his car and stand solemnly at a grave, far down the hill from me. His teenage niece had committed suicide. I had met him before, just after it had happened.

He had said to me in a kind way the day I met him, "I don't mean to take away from your grief, but I wish she would have died in a car wreck. At least that way it would make sense." I wasn't offended, I knew what he meant. Suicide would also be worse.

I heard about a wreck after Stephen's in which a passenger was decapitated. I remember thinking numbly *Stephen is just as dead as if he were decapitated,* but now I thank God that he wasn't, I thank God that I was able to view his body and that it wasn't any worse than it was.

I suppose it is a form of healing to realize that things could be worse. I thought again of the Garth Brooks song, *The Dance* and I stood to look at Stephen's picture. I could have missed the pain, but there's no way I would have missed the years God gave me with Stephen. I kissed his picture and left for home.

I know I'm doing better and I'm proud to be doing better, but I don't claim to be *over it.* I'll never be *over it.* Time does not heal all wounds. People die from wounds if the bleeding isn't stopped. Others learn to live with wounds, sometimes in a very handicapped state. The limp doesn't go away. Time eases the pain somewhat, but, in this case, it does not heal.

I flinch and always will flinch when I see a Ford Ranger truck. I'll never be able to look at one and see a whole truck. I'll always see that horribly demolished one and know what I lost.

But when I think back on my broken body beside the washer, I see myself as *crawling* to get to Stephen's pictures, as one would with a horrible wound. Of course, I was really walking. Now I *know* I'm walking and I'm proud to be walking.

At first, I was sure what I was going through would kill me and I didn't care. I was sure that an artery wall would be weakened by my pounding blood or that my heart would be weakened from the stress. No matter how many years it was before I died, this would be the cause.

I was sure that if I died in a car wreck, it would be because I was thinking about Stephen and not paying attention. In other words, I was sure the cause of death on my death certificate would read *losing Stephen*.

Now I know that when I go, it will be because it's my time to go. If it is from one of the things mentioned—if an artery wall was indeed weakened by my pounding blood or if my heart was damaged from the stress—that's just the way it was supposed to be. That's the way I was supposed to go. We all have to go one way or the other and we all go soon enough. I need to be here right now.

In February, Bradley, a little boy one month shy of his eighth birthday, was placed in the mausoleum, very close to Stephen. When I saw the flowers and realized how young he was, I stood and cried. I thought of Stephen at the age of eight and cried more. I respected this mother's grief before I ever met her.

Bradley had died of cancer. One of the first things his broken mother told me was that she just wanted to die. I knew not to say much right away, just seeing another mother breathe after losing a child is sometimes a testimony in itself to the next one who has to deal with it. I found that out when my aunt and my friend who had lost their sons walked into the funeral home.

Sometimes it's hard at first to listen, even if you are talking to someone who has lost a child. You think, *this was my child and it's different.* Of course, it is. Every circumstance is different and every parent thinks they loved their child more than the next parent. You can't imagine anyone loving a child the way you did yours. But they did and their grief needs to be respected. Not competed with, but respected.

This is where the half empty—half full glass comes in. When one looks at a glass with liquid to the halfway mark, it's a matter of choice to say the glass is half empty or half full. It's either, obviously.

The first time I met the parents of the forty four year old woman who had been shot, I felt such sympathy for them, I could scarcely contain the tears. I thought about the way the father had found the daughter, the anger they must feel toward the husband who shot her and I told them how sorry I was. The mother simply said, "Honey I'm so sorry about your son. I looked at his picture, he looks like such a sweet person. I realize I was allowed to have my daughter so much longer. I'm so sorry."

There was dignity in what she said. She was counting her blessings. The glass was half full, not half empty. She was thankful for the forty four years she had been given with her daughter. There was a lesson there for me.

I learned to count my blessings. I thanked God I had been able to have Stephen until he was eighteen. What a change from the year before when I was incredibly angry that Stephen had only lived to be eighteen. I'm also very thankful that I never saw him suffer. I didn't get to say goodbye, but I wouldn't have wanted him to suffer even long enough for me to get to him.

Yet I have run into people who have lost children and others to illnesses and they say that even though it was hard to watch their loved ones go through chemotherapy and operations, it was their time to say goodbye. This is their half full glass.

Wanting to own the title of worst possible situation is not healthy. If you win, you've made yourself the winner. And it shouldn't be a coveted prize. Sure, you can have the sympathy of the world, but what does that give you? I'd rather be a survivor and try to help someone else do the same.

CHAPTER TWELVE

A Year and a Half Later

A year and a half later, I can see that Stephen dying wasn't my fault. Aside from the fact earlier realized that there was nothing I could have done to deserve this kind of punishment, I can see his death for what it was. The law of deceleration. A human body can't take it, it can't go from thirty five or forty miles an hour to zero in a split second without sustaining a lot of injuries.

A year and a half later, I watch kids that Stephen played little league football with start to play college football at Georgia Tech and other colleges. I know that I could be bitter, hurt and angry, but I choose to see it as Stephen living on through those teammates.

A year and a half later, I can look at the picture in my bedroom of the mother and little boy and smile at all it meant to both of us.

A year and a half later, there are *nights* when I miss him so badly, I cry, and I wonder if he has certain times when he misses me the same way.

A year and a half later, there are *mornings* I miss him so badly, I cry silently into my bath towel. I emerge from the bathroom, no one finding me out. Sometimes it's just between Stephen and me. Sometimes it's just me. I know he's fine, happy beyond belief to have found the divine love he was so afraid he wouldn't be accepted into, and yet I still cry because I'm selfish. I miss him.

A year and a half later, I can hear an old song and I can sometimes cheat the pain by letting the song take me back to a time before the pain, when the song was new and my mother was running from the preacher with her shorts on.

Sometimes I can't. Sometimes I still have to relinquish the reprieve to the feeling that has haunted me now some million times or more. *He wasn't even born and you were eleven or twelve or fourteen or however old at the time this song was popular.* I fight the voice now, telling it that my chores aren't through, that I have a job to do here and Stephen has a job to do in Heaven and that's just the way it is.

A year and a half later, I glimpse a teenager, wearing a black Nike cap backward, baggy jeans, big black Nike tennis shoes. I know it's not Stephen, but I pretend it is. I stand and watch the teenager walk away; I hope he doesn't turn to face me, so I won't see unfamiliar features. Instead, I pretend that if he did turn toward me, I'd see that familiar smile, those straight teeth, those thick eyebrows shading his blue eyes, laughter just beneath the smile, as always.

A year and a half later, I know I will never stop missing Stephen. I think about when Daddy died and the two of us stayed in the living room all night those two nights. I remember Ron saying, "I heard the two of you talking and I knew it was the best therapy for both of you, so I left you alone." He was right. He was aware that I needed Stephen as much as Stephen needed me.

A year and a half later, I realize more than ever what a wonderful husband I have. He has stood beside me through thick and thin from the day I met him. And—I met him just a few weeks before my dad had the stroke. He was beside me with Nathan and Kristin in tow whether it was a school night or not, helping my family make very difficult decisions.

I know wonderful husbands are hard to come by and I will never take him for granted. He has been very patient and I know I have put him through so much during my grieving. I sainted Stephen and left Ron in the cold so many times.

A year and a half later, I can cry for Daddy. I walked into Pep Boys to buy a part for Stephanie's car and the smell that hit me when I walked in the door promised pain. I was puzzled. Rubbery, oily smells did not remind me of Stephen.

The cashier told me the price of the part and my eyes fell on a box of spark plugs about the same time. Daddy. I remembered all the times he had changed the spark plugs in my car, replaced wires and carburetors and God knows what else because I didn't drive new cars then and he tried to look out for me.

Tears filled my eyes and the girl probably thought I was upset about the price. I wasn't. It was a great price. What she didn't know and would never understand even if I told her was that I felt relief that I could cry for Daddy. Korea, Pork Chop Hill, the cigar he always had in his mouth. Daddy. I barely made it out the door before the tears turned to racking sobs. I can cry for Daddy now.

A year and a half later, I go away on trips, I have a good time. I rush to the mausoleum when I return with some trinket from the trip to hang from Stephen's flower vase. I kiss his picture repeatedly. I think as I kiss it how sad it is that I can't kiss him and I can't give him the souvenir and see him smile.

A year and a half later, the magnets on the refrigerator are like a smile from Stephen, saying, hey, Mama, remember when?

A year and a half later, I can take a deep breath without it hurting.

A year and a half later, I know that my original desperate feeling of he's gone from me forever was incorrect. The bond of a mother and child are not broken when that child dies. I still feel him beside me, encouraging me to go on and looking out for me, my very own guardian angel.

A year and a half later, I know my aunt was right. I am able to laugh and live again.

A year and a half later, I realize that God does know where you are, where you need to be and how to get you there.

A year and a half later, I see a church sign that says you can make your life a mess or a message. I pray that I can do the latter.

A year and a half later, I remember the way Stephen hugged me. His arms outstretched, reaching around my neck. I had seen him hug girls, his dear sweet Katie, the first love of his life. He would grab her in a bear hug, he would cling to her, hold her close to him, his arms around her waist. But he hugged me so sweetly, the exact way he had hugged me when he was four years old. It was so precious to me.

A year and a half later, I know that true sadness is to lose the heart of a child who is still on this earth. I know my son died loving me.

A year and a half later, I know that grief is not measured in tears shed or how many times one goes to the cemetery. People grieve in different ways and should never be judged for what they are or are not doing. Crying helps to release some of the pain and frustration, so no one should be told to stop crying. Others may prefer to cry alone and not share their grief. Sometimes the grief is strictly between the one gone on and the one left. No one should be condemned for not crying.

It should never be assumed that because a person is not crying that they are not hurting and didn't care as much about the one they lost. Condemning and judging and second guessing what a person is feeling or should be feeling is very unfair and very unnecessary.

The sad bottom line is that no matter how many tears are shed or how many hours are spent at the cemetery, the loved one doesn't come back. A way to go on must be found.

A year and a half later, my smile is my prize, my gift from God for having survived. I have fought hard to have it, I have earned it, and I will apologize to no one for it. Because I smile does not mean I hurt less than the next person.

A year and a half later, I wonder if I will ever get used to not hearing his alarm clock in the mornings or his footsteps on the stairs in the evenings. I long to hear his laughter and I think I always will.

A year and a half later, I will echo my son's question, what would the world be without music? I love it to the depths of my soul, despite any preacher's or anyone else's opinion of it.

A year and a half later, I hear Elton John's song, *Recover Your Soul*, and I know that I have recovered mine. It was missing in action for a while. I take comfort where I can find it and I find it in Elton John, a man who sang *Crocodile Rock* in a carefree manner when I was a teenager, then came to me with a serious suggestion in my time of crisis. *Hey now, let's recover your soul.*

A year and a half later, I realize that many, many people have suffered great loss and they have survived. And I think the person who has passed on would want nothing less.

A year and a half later, I remember driving into the Alps with Stephen and his beloved Uncle Tim. Tim was in the Army and stationed in Germany. Being a snow starved Georgia girl, I marveled at the snow that seemed to have a thousand diamonds trapped inside it, sparkling magnificently as the sun touched it.

The mountains grew larger and larger, more majestic as we climbed, the snow getting deeper. *Wow*, Stephen said as Tim took the car around a curve and more mountains loomed ahead. *This is only the foothills*, Tim said. *You ain't seen nothing yet.*

No way, Stephen said. But Tim was right.

I believe life is only the foothills. Just as Stephen and I couldn't imagine the grandeur that was to come in the Alps, I still can't imagine the grandeur of Heaven. Stephen went on to explore that before me. I truly believe we *ain't seen nothing yet.*

A few days beyond a year and a half later, I watch John Glenn blast off into space once again. I am fully aware that I was in second grade when he went up the first time and that Stephen wasn't even born. That day in February of 1962 seems like another lifetime. I wonder momentarily why I have been here long enough to look back and remember an event that happened thirty six years ago and Stephen was only here a total of eighteen years.

I smile at the hero John Glenn is, I have patriotic tears in my eyes as the shuttle lifts off. Then I realize that my son is as much a hero to me as John Glenn is to the world. I remember another famous person, Bill Cosby, looking into the camera on a cold day in January of 1997 and saying, *My son was my hero.* His son who had just been murdered. The appropriateness of his words stunned me even then, three months before I had lost a child. They mean even more to me now and I hope Mr. Cosby doesn't mind if I echo his words, *My son was my hero.*

A little over a year and a half later, Ron and I proceed with buying land to build a new house, something we were actively pursuing when Stephen died. It, along with many other things, had been put on hold. One of our soon to be neighbors asked me how many children we had. I said, as I always do, "I have two children from my first marriage and I gained two with the second marriage." She nodded and said *same with us.*

I thought of how nice it would be to really still have all of those children alive and envied her for a moment. *She's going to be your neighbor, Marcia,* I told myself. *Maybe you should clarify.* "I say I have two children from the first marriage because I will always feel that I do, but, actually, my youngest died in a car wreck," I confessed.

Tears came to her eyes. "So did mine," she said. Her son had died nine months before mine. I look forward to being her neighbor. I think maybe God planned it that way.

The house we are building will not have a room that is *Stephen's room.* There will be no shrine, however there are so many things of Stephen's that I'll never part with. His room in our current house unintentionally became my writing room after he died. I felt close to him in the room and I wrote peacefully, sitting on his futon.

I will have a separate room in the new house that is my writing room and the futon will go with me to that room. So will the shelf that holds his football, basketball and baseball trophies, his rock collection, his favorite books, many pictures of him and souvenirs we collected from different places. I have a hope chest full of his clothes. They still smell like him.

I have his Nintendo trunk, Mario running across it. He used it to store Nintendo games in when he was twelve. I have it full of secret treasures—his wrestling figures, his Star Wars figures, little Hot Wheel cars, a little Gremlin shirt that he wore when he was five, to name just a few. I usually have manuscript scattered across the top of both the hope chest and the trunk, but sometimes, I move all that paper and I open the hope chest or the trunk and I smile as I touch those things. I laugh that one of the wrestlers was just elected governor of Minnesota and I can imagine Stephen's laughter.

A little over a year and a half later, I know that I don't have to trade memories for the relief of the pain. My pain has become a dull ache over a year and a half and my memories are still vivid. As much as I play those memories over and over in my head, I know they aren't going anywhere. Stephen will always be a part of my life, the memories he left me will always be a part of my smile.

A little over a year and a half later, I see flowers once again on the side of the mausoleum where Stephen is. One flat blanket of flowers says *Son*. My heart hurts. I look at the birthday on the white piece of paper that is taped to the crypt until the marker can be obtained. 1956. I was born in 1955. I guessed that his parents would be in their sixties or seventies. It doesn't matter how old they are. A blanket of flowers that says the word *Son* or *Daughter* is an item a parent should never have to buy.

I'm sure there's a reason and someday, when I have the big picture, perhaps I'll understand. But a year and a half later, I do not understand why anyone has to endure the kind of pain that losing a child brings.

A little over a year and a half later, I never again make just a donation when someone dies. I dig deeper in my wallet and send an arrangement of flowers as well. I'll never forget what the flowers meant. Most charities are around all year and if I truly care about the organization's welfare, I can contribute more money to it anytime I want, not just when someone dies.

House plants and potted plants that can be replanted outside are not only a lasting reminder that someone shared your grief with you, but therapeutic for the person taking care of them. The garden I planted with flowers from Stephen's baskets gave me something to do with my hands in my zombie state. The beautiful garden it became is a tribute to Stephen as well as to my survival.

Each time I see a new bloom, I know that a caring soul gave that flower to show their love for Stephen, that I wasn't alone in that horrible time. Flowers are a priceless act, no matter the size of the arrangement.

A little over a year and a half later, construction begins to enclose the mausoleum. I view it with mixed emotions. I know now that Stephen is not cold or hot, that he is not really there. I think maybe it was selfish of me to want him inside, so I think of moving him so he will still be outside.

Yet I feel discomfort at the thought of unsealing the crypt, having the coffin pulled out and placed in another crypt.

Many people are doing it, some with ceremonies and this is the right thing for them. If I were to lay eyes on that coffin again, knowing his body is inside it, the physical aspect of it would bring an emotional storm to me. Emotional storms still come my way. They are not as frequent, but they are just as intense when they hit. Some can't be avoided. Some can. I will leave the coffin where it is.

A little over a year and a half later, it's still *hard to hold together in the cold November Rain.* I pull the Christmas decorations out of our storage shed, the November rain truly cold as it hits me in the face. I think of the pain mingled with joy that my ornaments bring to me.

Each year of their lives as children, Stephanie, Stephen and I created ornaments and placed their pictures inside. Many years it was *make it bake its*, other years we painted ceramic ornaments to hold the pictures. One year Stephen made an ornament holder at school, a Mason jar lid wrapped with red yarn. I knew I would stare at it as I had the year before, knowing that his little hands had wound that string. He was six and a tooth was missing in the picture. It would bring to mind Secret Santa shops and gifts he had bought me there.

One year Stephen created an ornament with paper, scissors and crayons and chose the picture of himself with our old English sheepdog to grace his masterpiece. He was seven. There is a dough Santa he made at school and a bell made from aluminum foil and a Dixie cup that he made in the church nursery. They bring me joy and they bring me pain.

I remind myself that there are felt candy canes that Stephanie made for me when she was five, there are adorable pictures of her without teeth, there are beautiful pictures of her as a teenager and there are new ornaments of her and her beautiful twins and there are ornaments of Nathan and Kristin.

I work with determination, loading the tree down with ornaments, trying not to give in to depression. I have always celebrated Christmas a full thirty days and I will continue that tradition. I think of how unfair it would be for Lauren and Brittany to come to my house at Christmas, no cookies being made, no huge tree to decorate. They would say to each other, *"Remember before Uncle 'tephen died when Mimi used to make cookies with us and decorate gingerbread men and we helped hang ornaments on her tree?"*

There will be none of that. I will celebrate Christmas the way I always have, Stephen's ornaments will always be on the tree, though it will always tear at my heart that he is not physically with us.

I will take heart in the excitement in Lauren and Brittany and Kristin's eyes as they decorate cookies and hang ornaments and Stephen will be proud of me. Kristin will be in the Christmas pageant at church and Lauren and Brittany will marvel at the spectacular nativity scene and Baby Jesus. They will sing *Away in a Manger* until February.

I will not look back on the year of 1998 as a sad and lonely year, my first full year without Stephen. I will look on it as a year when the warmth of people amazed me and made a difference in my life. I will remember the kindness so many people bestowed on me, people who were concerned for my well being, who truly cared about me and let me know it. I never knew and would have never chosen to find out in such a manner that so many people cared about me, but I am appreciative.

It will also be a year when I look back on the little miracle that was Stephen Beam, a child who taught me how to deal with co-workers, parents, even boy friends and the rest of the world in general. A child who believed in himself and lived life the way he saw fit to do it, not bending and conforming to please others.

His earring and long hair represented who he was and he trusted in that, though many would have had him change it. He taught me to believe in myself. I had lived my life to try and please everyone else and he knew it. He made it clear to me that it was important not to do that.

A little over a year and a half later, I will cherish every moment I was allowed to have with Stephen, every yesterday when we talked, laughed and were able to stand within inches of each other. Though it hurts that I can't stand within inches of him now and carry on a conversation and watch him laugh at things I say, or touch him, I will still live my life for today and look forward to tomorrow and all that it may bring. I'm sure there will be more nieces and nephews, more grandchildren, maybe even great grandchildren. Maybe I will be able to touch their lives, to make this world a better place for them somehow.

No matter how many grandchildren I may have, I will always know that there's a missing little Stephen Bo Jackson Beam. He won't smile at me with Stephen's mischievous eyes, he won't come running in the door and up the steps, happy to be at his Mimi's house, the way the others do. And his dad, the grown up Stephen, I'll never know in this world.

I sometimes wonder if Stephen will be all grown up in Heaven or if he'll still be that laughing eighteen year old. I also wonder if when I die, Stephen will come walking over that hill, motioning me on with a smile, the way he did at Disney World or Kennedy Space Center. I think he will. I think he will walk toward me smiling, helping me make the transition into a world he's already accustomed to. He'll show me the way in that world that has its base just on the other side of Stephen's Moon.

Epilogue

On January 23, 1998, Robin, my sister-in law from my first marriage and her husband Mike, brought a beautiful little boy into the world. His name is Austin. I heard his first cries, I held him when he was just minutes old. He will call me Mimi. An hour or so after he was born, he struggled to free his hand of the tightly wrapped blanket the nurses had bound him in and he grasped my finger. It was as if he were saying, *I'm here. I'll enrich your life if you let me.*

He is a happy little boy, pleasant and easy going, his spirit so like Stephen. I love him and he loves me.

On January 16, 1999, Stephen's Uncle Tim, my brother in law from my first marriage, and his wife, Sherry, added another little boy to the family. This little boy's name is Stephen Beam. He, too, will call me Mimi. Tim says the name is their salute to my Stephen. It is a very worthy salute. The child warms my heart. He has big eyes that look seriously into mine and he has the shoulders of a future football player—or baseball player—or both maybe, like Bo Jackson. I can only think as I smile at the precious little namesake that there *will* be a little Stephen 'Bo Jackson' Beam running up the stairs, happy to be at his Mimi's house.

Stephen will be proud of me for surviving,

Marcia